SOMERSET

SHOCKING, SURPRISING and STRANGE

Jack W Sweet

HALSGROVE

First published in Great Britain in 2023

Copyright © Jack W Sweet

All rights reserved. No part of this publication may be reproduced, stored in a retrieval system, or transmitted in any form or by any means without the prior permission of the copyright holder.

British Library Cataloguing-in-Publication Data
A CIP record for this title is available from the British Library

ISBN 978 0 85704 359 7

Halsgrove
Halsgrove House,
Ryelands Business Park,
Bagley Road, Wellington, Somerset TA21 9PZ
Tel: 01823 653777 Fax: 01823 216796
email: sales@halsgrove.com

Part of the Halsgrove group of companies
Information on all Halsgrove titles is available at: www.halsgrove.com

Printed and bound in India by Parksons Graphics Ltd

CONTENTS

Introduction	6
Three Shocking Murders	7
The Bread Riots of 1867	11
Mary Adlam Kills Her Drunken Husband	13
James Martin's Watery Adventure	17
Drinking at Martock	19
Mr Hardwicke Fights Back	21
The Ice Broke	23
The Killing on Midford Hill	25
Tragic Drowning Tragedies.	29
A Poet a Navigator and a Deadly Encounter	33
The Yeovil Smallpox Hospital	36
Big Bangs	42
The Wyvern's Down!	44
Highway Robbery	47
Somewhat Shocking, Surprising, and Strange	50
The Battle Of Langport	53
Car Thieves	57
Alias Blue Jemmy	60
Aviation Thrills and Spills	62
And It Was All For a Kiss	64
Crazy Rides	66
Fire at Dunster	68
The Port for Yeovil	72
Death Rode The Skimmington	76
At Random	79
Mr Edginton's Mistake	82
A Shocking Autumn Storm	84
Breakfast at Coombe Villa	88
Death at Ilchester Gaol	90

The Tragic Death of Gunner Sims	92
A Battle With Poachers	94
All Guns Are Dangerous	97
Thomas Pearce is Shot	100
A Tragedy in the River Yeo	102
Death at Deadman's Post	104
A Friend and a Foe	106
A Long Forgotten Ghost Story	108
Fire!	110
Lost at Sea	113
A Turbulent Year	116
The Reckleford School Riot of 1921	118
A Day at the Somerset Winter Assizes	121
'Lawrence of the RAF'	124
Thieves and Quarrels	127
The Missing Ballot Papers	129
Briefly Shocking and Surprising	131
Captain Hunt Goes on the Run	134
Death in the Coal Pit	137
The Yeovil Cheese Robbery and Other Cases	141
And Finally, the Last Surprise	143
Sources	144
Acknowledgements	144

DEDICATION

This book is dedicated to the memory of
my late wife Margaret who so willingly
persevered and supported me during
my many excursions into the past of my
home town of Yeovil and my native county
of Somerset, the delightful and historic
Land of Summer.

INTRODUCTION

In his 1881 *Tourist's guide to Somerset-Rail and Road,* R.N. Worth FGS wrote that '... there was little that is grand, but much that is beautiful. There are meadows where cattle graze-knee deep in grass, wide vales, barren rolling hills, wide tablelands crested with the richest foliage, broken by valleys in which the comfortable farmhouses nestle snugly amidst orchards which in spring burst into veritable seas of blossom. For scenes of loveliness, Somerset may challenge any county in England.'

This is my fifth book on the theme of 'Shocking, Surprising and rather Strange' stories found beneath those 'scenes of loveliness'.

A lane near Dunster but beneath such peaceful Somerset scenes could lurk shocking, surprising and sometimes strange events.

THREE SHOCKING MURDERS

Thomas Laver of Ilton was a very careful man and saved for his old age from his meagre labourer's wages. In fact, he was so careful that it was said that 'by hard labour and a most penurious mode of living (frequently eating with hogs) he had accumulated nearly 40 pounds in cash which he always carried about with him sewn up in his pockets'. Thomas Laver's fortune was so well known in the area that no one was very surprised when one evening in December 1798 he was found battered to death, his pockets cut open and his money gone.

Suspicion fell on two local villains, Richard Williams and James Podger, who had been overheard saying that they would not mind killing Thomas Laver for his money and who had now disappeared from their usual haunts. Warrants were issued for their arrest and a month later a letter was intercepted from James Podger to his relatives in Ilton asking for his box of clothes and some money to be sent to a public house at Mile End Green in London.

The murdered Thomas Laver lies at peace in the churchyard of St Peter's, Ilton.

The Ilminster postmaster and a local gentleman accompanied the box to London where they sought the assistance of the Bow Street Magistrates to effect the arrests. Two Bow Street Runners, the postmaster and his companion, Podger's box and a third Runner disguised as a porter made their way to the public house. The 'porter' entered and was met by Richard Williams who confirmed that his friend James Podger was expecting the box and on being identified by the postmaster was arrested. Shortly after Podger arrived back at the public house and was taken into custody. Despite both men vehemently denying any knowledge or involvement with the murder, the Bow Street Magistrates were satisfied with the evidence of identification given by the Ilminster postmaster and his companion, and the accused were committed to prison pending their return to Somerset.

Only Richard Williams stood trial at the Somerset Assizes charged with the murder of Thomas Laver – James Podger had turned King's Evidence and escaped the fate of his erstwhile companion who was found guilty and sentenced to death.

Richard Williams was hanged in April 1799 at Ilton acknowledging the justice of his sentence and James Podger disappeared into the mist of time.

Farmer Styling was tired as he returned home to his farm in the small village of Goathurst, near Bridgwater, late in the evening of Wednesday 15 November 1809. After a long day helping a neighbour sow his wheat, he was looking forward to supper in the warm farmhouse kitchen. However, as Farmer Styling entered the yard, he was puzzled to find the barn doors wide open, and going into the house, was horrified to find his twenty-seven-year-old wife, Sarah, lying on the kitchen floor in a mess of smashed crockery and blood, dead. The shocked farmer also found that his young farm servant Thomas Gage had disappeared and his mare was missing from the stable. A search of the farmhouse discovered the theft of two £10 notes, some silver coins and spoons, a great coat, some dresses and a gun with powder and shot. A closer examination of Sarah's body revealed that she had been killed by a vicious blow by an axe or hatchet to the back of her head as she sat at the kitchen table.

The hue and cry was raised for the murderer and robber, and within a short time the farmer's mare, much driven and minus saddle and bridle, was found grazing quietly on Brendon Hill. Two days later, the missing farm servant was discovered hiding near his parent's home in the Exmoor village of Brompton Regis, and it was established that Thomas Gage was in fact, Thomas Tarr, who had absconded from his apprenticeship in the village during the previous June. However, none of the stolen cash or articles was found with him.

Thomas Tarr was brought back to Goathurst and examined by the local magistrates. Pleading his innocence of the crime, Tarr stated that some little while before he had been riding a horse owned by Mrs Styling's father and had driven the animal so hard that it had fallen and subsequently died. His mistress had threatened to send him to gaol, and on the afternoon of the murder, he saw two men come into the farmyard. Fearing they had come to take him to gaol, Tarr explained that he had fled from the barn where he had been working and made his way to his home. He suggested that the men might have been the murderers and robbers. In the fall from the horse, Tarr had hurt his leg, but the examining magistrates were not convinced that he could have walked the many miles to Brompton Regis with such an injury. Neither were they convinced that he was telling the truth, and he was committed to Ilchester Gaol to await his trial at the next Somerset Assizes.

On Monday, 2 April 1810, eighteen-years-old Thomas Gage, alias Tarr, appeared at the Somerset Spring Assizes in Taunton, and was found guilty of the murder of his mistress, Sarah Styling, and then robbing her house, and sentenced to death. Seven days later the young murderer was hanged at the Stone Gallows, near Taunton, having confessed his guilt a few hours before the fatal drop.

Mr Metford of Glastonbury, woollen stocking manufacturer, employed out workers in Wells and the area around the city, and every Saturday, Robert Parsons delivered the wool and collected and paid for the finished stockings. On Saturday, 10 December 1815, Robert Parsons, with the help of James Marsh, another of Mr Metford's employees, loaded up the covered delivery cart with the bags of wool and placed the £12 cash for the wages by his driver's seat. Just before he was about to leave, James Marsh, who had been sent to feed his employer's cattle, came running up and asked the carter if he could ride with him to Wells. No objection was raised and they set off for the city.

Halfway between Glastonbury and Wells, some labourers were at work in a brickyard, when they heard the faint shouts and sounds of a struggle coming from a covered cart they could see some way off on the high road.

As the cart travelled on towards Wells, the sounds of the struggle became more violent and were followed by the loud shrieks and groans of someone in great distress. The workmen dropped their tools and went to render assistance, but as they approached the cart they saw a man dragging an apparently lifeless body from the vehicle and into the roadside ditch. Shouting 'murder' the men ran towards the cart, and the supposed assassin jumped over the hedge and made off across the fields as fast as he could run. The workmen found Robert Parsons lying dead in the ditch, badly beaten and with his throat shockingly cut from ear to ear. Whilst several of the men remained with the body, one of them went in pursuit of the fleeing figure, and just recognised the fugitive before he lost sight of him behind some hayricks; it was James Marsh whom he had known since they were children.

James Marsh was quickly taken into custody and on Friday 5 April 1816, he appeared at the Somerset Spring Assizes in Taunton, charged with the murder of Robert Parsons. Marsh was found guilty and sentenced to hang at Ilchester Gaol on Monday 8 April following which his body would be sent for dissection.

The *Taunton Courier* reported on 11 April that:

'On the road from Taunton to Ilchester, Marsh behaved in a most hardened an audacious manner, and throughout that day was equally violent and abusive to all who came near him. On Sunday he appeared very unconcerned at chapel, but during that day he was less abusive. On depravity of human nature as any that ever stained the criminal annals of the county. On Monday he was visited early by the Rev. Mr Reece, chaplain to the gaol, to whom he acknowledged the crime for which he was to suffer, but declined assigning any motive for it. He appeared less insensible to his situation than before, but refused the sacrament. At nine, his brother-in-law was admitted to visit him, of whom he took leave in a very careless, unconcerned manner. At a quarter before eleven he was removed from the chapel, and on turning round to shake hands with his brother convicts appeared affected. From thence he proceeded to the platform, and as usual the chaplain first ascended the drop, the prisoner immediately followed, and had no sooner arrived there, then finding the chaplain about to call him to prayers, he said, "no, I shall say no more – where is the man" (meaning the executioner) "I am ready." He however was prevailed on to kneel down and join in prayer, but in less than three minutes he up in the middle of a prayer, and again called for the man. The chaplain descended, and the executioner got up to perform his sad office, during the performance of which the prisoner frequently said "make haste." He was however left about two minutes, when he again said "I am ready" and instantly fell. He died without a struggle. During the time the executioner was placing the rope around his neck the prisoner thought it was not properly placed and told the executioner to put it a little further back. Thus perished this desperate murderer in the 23rd year of his age.'

Although the motive for the murder was never publicly established, the *Western Flying Post* suggested that James Marsh was to have married the week after the murder was committed, and it was supposed that he meant to get the necessary cash by robbing and killing Robert Parsons.

THE BREAD RIOTS OF 1867

The towns and villages across South Somerset were angry in November 1867; food prices were very high and in particular, bread was now costing eightpence and more for a modest loaf. An agricultural worker would be lucky to receive wages of ten shillings a week, and a skilled worker, such as a glove cutter could expect to earn not much over a weekly wage of one pound. The eightpenny loaf was causing great hardship to many families and especially the poor.

People blamed local bakers for putting up the prices and anger exploded in Chard on the evening of Monday 11 November 1867. Men, women and children assembled in the town centre and reaching several hundred strong surged up Fore Street smashing in the process the shop windows of the street's two bakers' shops. As the crowd returned cheering and shouting past the town hall, the mayor, Councillor Salter, came out onto the balcony and making himself heard above the din called for them to go home because what they were doing was against the law and useless. Surprisingly it seems that the mayor saved the day because the crowd dispersed and drifted home; by midnight the town was quiet.

From the balcony of Chard Town Hall, the mayor Councillor Salter urged the crowd to go home.

However, fearing a repeat during the following evening, 40 county policemen were drafted in to patrol the town supported by a large number of local special constables, and although a crowd gathered in Fore Street, after much cheering and shouting the assembly broke up and everyone went home.

There was no further trouble in Chard, the policemen left early on Wednesday morning and the specials stood down.

The news of Monday's turmoil in Chard soon spread across South Somerset and on Tuesday evening several hundred people assembled in the Market Square at Ilminster. There was much shouting, cheering and singing and before long stones were thrown at the door of a butcher's shop and two bakers' shop windows shattered by stones. Strange as it might seem, the only two police constables remaining in the town following the departure of the sergeant and ten officers to Chard, managed to break up the crowd and there was no further trouble in Ilminster during the rest of the week.

At Castle Cary, the price of a loaf of well over eightpence brought out the crowds for three evenings, but despite much sound and fury no property was damaged, and when the local bakers reduced the price of a loaf down to eightpence on Thursday evening the town quickly returned to normal.

Yeovil's turn came on Wednesday 13 November when during the evening a large crowd gathered in the Borough and demanded the reduction in bread prices. The town police sergeant and several constables calmed the passions but as the crowd dispersed there were shouts of 'We'll be back tomorrow night.'

Thus warned a small army of special constables was sworn in and when the crowd assembled on the following evening they were met by the local police and specials. Overawed by the show of strength, the crowd dispersed peaceably and the rest of the week was trouble-free.

The most serious disturbance was at South Petherton on the Thursday evening, when about three hundred people, many armed with bludgeons and heavy hammers, assembled at Pitney and marched to the Bell Inn smashing shop windows on the way. The local police sergeant and four men were knocked aside and Mr Banfield's shop windows were smashed as were those of Mr Ashman's bakery. Following an attack on more shop windows, the police were assaulted again as they tried to restore law and order. A full-scale riot was now in progress, shops and houses were damaged and the cry went out to go and smash up Mr Banfield's flour mill. However, Mr Banfield saved his mill by liberally supplying the rioters with bread, cheese and cider as a reward for not doing so!

The riot lasted over three hours and was finally brought to an end by the arrival of some 40 special constables armed with batons who broke up the mob, arrested the ringleaders and took them into custody. There was no further trouble in South Petherton.

At the following January Somerset Quarter Sessions in Taunton, nineteen men and boys were found guilty of riot and assault at South Petherton and sentenced to between one and six months hard labour

On the following Monday, a crowd of women assembled in Bruton's main street, but after a great deal of shouting they all went home,

The last flare-up was at Stoke-sub-Hamdon where a group of youths marched out to Montacute shouting and cheering, but as they could find no one from the village to join them, they marched noisily back home.

The was no further trouble in this part of Somerset, the price of bread remained high and the poor gritted their teeth and carried on.

MARY ADLAM KILLS HER DRUNKEN HUSBAND

Mrs Mary Adlam worked hard to make a living making straw hats at her shop in Regency Bath, and her husband Mr Henry Adlam drank hard on the profits.

Wednesday 18 May 1814, did not start well in the Adlam household in the shop on Bath Street because Mr Adlam was in his usual intoxicated state. And in this condition, he was prone to violence. The strong words between the husband and wife ended with Mr Adlam calling Mary a bitch and a whore, banged her head several times against the shop wall and raged out for another day's hard drinking.

Mary recovered, as usual, and with Sarah Ellis, her new apprentice began the daily task of making straw hats and bonnets for the fashionable ladies of Bath and to fuel Mr Adlam's passion for liquor.

Mary and her apprentice had just finished their afternoon tea and were about to clear the table in the parlour next to the shop when Mr Adlam returned, very drunk and demanded his tea. Because Mary wanted to use the parlour table for lining some bonnets, she asked her husband to have his tea downstairs in the kitchen. However, this was not to Mr Adams' liking and shouting that he was damned if he would and swearing that he would take his tea in the parlour, rang the bell violently to summon Betty Whitehead, the family servant from the kitchen.

However, Mary was determined to use the table and picked up the tray of cups but before she could hand it to the servant Mr Adlam snatched it away shouting that he would have his tea in the parlour, placed it on the sideboard and punched his wife to the floor calling her a blasted whore. Painfully she staggered to her feet only to be struck a savage blow accompanied by her husband yelling at her to go back to London and her friends as she was a blasted whore. Reeling from the parlour and across the shop, Mary collapsed behind the counter. Pulling herself up, distraught and in pain, she staggered back towards the parlour screaming that if her husband believed that she was a whore then why did he continue to live with her and let her support him. By now she was in a great passion and, fearing that her mistress would be beaten again, Betty Whitehead grabbed her around to waist to prevent her from going into the parlour.

Sweeping materials and hats from the counter Mr Adlam staggered across the shop swearing that he had not finished with his wife. From then on everything happened very quickly. Mary Adlam managed to return to the parlour but then came back into the shop carrying the large case knife she had been using to cut the bread at teatime. Waving the knife at her husband she dared him to repeat the accusations, which he did by calling her a damned blasted whore and lunged forward to strike her again. For a moment a mixture of fear and fury burned in Mary's heart, then down slashed the knife cutting the sleeve of her husband's jacket and she turned and rushed back into the parlour.

Looking down at his arm he exclaimed to the watching apprentice, 'She has cut me!' and as he stretched out his arm to show Sarah, blood began to pour from the sleeve. Horrified, Sarah cried out, 'Oh, Mr Adlam there is blood!' and called for her mistress who came hurrying back from the parlour. Gently, all anger spent Mary took her husband's arm and managed to persuade the rapidly sobering and now frightened man to go down to the kitchen. They managed the top two of the steep steps but then Mr Adlam stumbled and the couple crashed down the remaining fourteen treads landing heavily on the stone-flagged kitchen floor.

Mary Adlam and her husband would have been familiar with the Pump Room and the Old White Hart, shown here in Regency Bath.

The injured man was hauled fainting, by his wife and the servant onto a chair and Betty Whitehead tried unsuccessfully to stem the flow of blood. Surgeon Day who lived nearby was called and after bandaging the wound reassured Mr Adlam that it was not serious; twenty-four hours later thirty-years-old Mr Henry Adlam was dead and within another twenty-four, Mrs Mary Adlam was lodged in Ilchester Gaol charged with the capital offence of murdering her husband.

Three months later on 13 August 1814, Mrs Mary Ada Adlam appeared before the judge, Sir Vicary Gibbs, at the Somerset Assizes at Wells, and pleaded not guilty to the charge of wilful murder.

The apprentice, Sarah Ellis, was the principal witness and stated that she had lived with the Adlams for nine weeks before the fatal day, and had been learning the straw hat business. She had always found Mrs Adlam to be a 'tender humane woman' to her husband but often he was very drunk and then would be 'abusive and used the prisoner ill'. Sarah described the events of the 18 May but although she had witnessed the row and the beatings she had not seen her mistress cut Mr Adlam because at that moment she had been picking up silver paper from the floor behind the counter. She testified that Mr Adlam was very drunk at the time.

Next to give evidence was the servant, Betty Whitehead who stated that she had been in the Adlam's employ for about sixteen months and corroborated the evidence of Sarah Ellis. She said that her master was often drunk and was then abusive to his wife calling her a whore and other things. During the row at teatime, she had feared Mr Adlam would kill his wife. Betty went on to recall that she had heard him tell his wife not to trouble herself because it was all his fault.

The third witness was Elizabeth Figgis, a neighbour's servant who had been called to nurse Mr Adlam. At about nine o'clock the following morning the patient had complained that his stomach hurt and of being in pain all over. Surgeon Goldstone was called, and after examining Mr Adlam, pronounced that he was dying. Elizabeth Figgis went on to say that during the time she had nursed Mr Adlam he had repeatedly asked his wife not to grieve for his because it was his own fault and begged her to stay by his side and kiss him time and time again.

Mary Adlam now put forward her defence in writing and this was read to the court describing the 'the abuse and provocation received from her husband, and she was so irritated as not to be sensible of what she had done but concluded that in the height of her passion she must have given the fatal wound. She called upon God to witness the truth of her assertion and that she had no intention of doing him any harm'.

A number of witnesses now came forward to speak for Mrs Adlam, all of whom spoke highly of her character and affection for her husband. A neighbour, Miss Elizabeth Gardner stated that during the two years that she had known the accused she had found her to be 'a very virtuous, humane, good sort of woman, very affectionate to her husband, and endeavouring to prevail upon him to stay at home'. She had been present during the last few hours of Mr Adlam's life and recalled that the dying man had told her that he did not think that his wife had deliberately cut him. Just before he died Mr Adlam had embraced his wife, kissed her and whispered, 'Mary forgive me and make it up.'

Surgeon Goldstone and a colleague Surgeon Day, who also had attended Mr Adlam, testified that at first neither thought the wound to be of much consequence and suggested that his death was partly caused by falling down the stairs, partly by excessive drinking and partly by passion.

However, the judge, Sir Vicary Gibbs, was not satisfied with this vague testimony and told the medical men that they must confine themselves to one question – did they think that the wound caused the death? In reply, the surgeons prevaricated suggesting that the wound was aggravated by other circumstances.

The judge was still not satisfied and said that the question he posed was a very plain one and he must have a direct answer. If the deceased had not been wounded with a knife, would the fall down the stairs, the inflamed intoxicated state of his blood and the violent passion he was in, have caused his death? – Yes or No? The unanimous reply came 'Certainly not!'

Sir Vicary in his summing up to the jury, read over the evidence and advised that language no matter how foul and provocative, could not justify a person taking up a knife and dealing a mortal blow to a fellow-creature. But if they thought that the blow was struck whilst the quarrel between the prisoner and the deceased was high, the crime could be softened down to manslaughter. If, however, they thought there was a sufficient lapse of time whereby the prisoner could have recovered from the moment of passion, a verdict of wilful murder must be given. The jury only took a few minutes to return a verdict of Guilty to Manslaughter and Mary Adlam fainted. She fainted again when on her recovery, the judge sentenced her to six months imprisonment. The general register of Ilchester Gaol records that Mrs Mary Ada Adlam was discharged from the 'Common Gaol' on 13 February 1815 and disappears from the record.

JAMES MARTIN'S WATERY ADVENTURE

Across the West Country for three days in November 1894 it rained, from the 10th to the 12th it rained incessantly. Rivers overflowed their banks, the Levels were underwater and all across Somerset many towns and villages were badly flooded.

One of the worst affect towns was Langport where within hours the River Parrett overflowed the embankments and Bow Street resembled a canal with boats being sailed up and down. As well as inundating all the houses, pubs and shops of Bow Street, the gasworks was put out of action and traffic on the railway going through Langport came to a standstill. No one in the town, even the oldest inhabitants, could remember such flooding. The flat moorland around Langport was described as resembling a vast inland sea.

In Yeovil, the lower parts of the town suffered extensive flooding of houses and several glove factories adjoining the Mill Stream below Addlewell Lane suffered flood damage. For fear of their steam locomotives' fires being extinguished by the deep floodwater on the lines between Yeovil Pen Mill Station and Marston Magna, the Great Western Railway cancelled all train services. The road from Mudford to Marston Magna was nearly 7 feet (about two metres) underwater. However, floods or not, carrier James Martin, being of a stubborn disposition was not going to be prevented from carrying out his rounds, and so he set out with his horse van from Yeovil to deliver groceries, drapery and gloves to South Petherton and the surrounding villages. Accompanying James was a passenger by name of Clark *en route* to Shepton Beauchamp.

The wreckage of James Martin's cart with the dead horse still in harness.

To reach South Petherton James had to cross Shores Bridge which spanned the River Parrett but because the river had broken its banks, the road on the Yeovil side of the bridge was underwater. However, James Martin decided to attempt to cross but as he drove his heavily laden van along the flooded road the violent current swept the feet from under the horse, the van tipped and the animal and the vehicle were caught in the torrent. Trees and the roadside bank prevented the horse and van together with its occupants from being swept into the river and drowned. Even so, the poor horse did not survive but James and his companion managed to cling to the cart, shouting for help. And help was at hand.

George Wines who had witnessed the event raised the alarm with Major W Blake, his employer at Bridge House, and together with Mr Jones who was visiting the Major, they began the rescue operations. At first, they tried to drive a horse and cart into the flood but were driven back by the violence of the torrent. Major Blake and Mr Jones then decided to wade into the swirling water at great personal risk and got close enough to throw a rope to the cold, wet desperate men. After several attempts, Clarke the passenger, finally caught the rope and the two were pulled to safety. Both were in a complete state of exhaustion but despite being plied with hot drinks and wrapped in warm blankets, James Martin was nowhere near recovery. He was taken to the Bell Inn at South Petherton where after several days he made a full recovery and returned home to his wife and family and with the loss of the valuable horse and van, his business.

Shores Bridge was replaced in the 1970s with a modern bridge on the dual carriageway A303.

DRINKING AT MARTOCK

In 1860, the County Petty Sessions were held in Yeovil but dealt with offences committed outside the town boundaries. On Wednesday 1 February 1860, Giles Gaylard appeared before the Bench summoned for being drunk in Martock on the previous 7 January. PC Marshman stated that he was on duty at about one o'clock in the morning and came up to the defendant who was with a number of friends and who was very drunk. As he passed the group, Giles Gaylard became abusive but when the constable told him to go home quietly, he had used abusive and offensive expressions.

Mr Jolliffe, the solicitor acting for Giles Gaylard, went on the attack, and demanded to know how the constable knew his client to be drunk and did he judge this to be from his own experience? PC Marshman replied that did not know what the solicitor meant. Mr Jolliffe, continued with this line of questioning and enquired whether in the constable's opinion his client was in the same state as he, the witness, had been in at a recent sale? The constable protested that he had not been under the influence of drink on that occasion and went on to say that the defendant had been shouting 'There's no chance for the bobby tonight.' Mr Jolliffe then asked the policeman whether Giles Gaylard had told him that 'You had better try and find out serious offences and protect the property of parishioners than go about eaves-dropping and creating unpleasantness between neighbours.' PC Marshman confirmed this, and stated that the defendant went on to taunt him by

This quiet scene in Martock is in contrast with the noisy revelry of 7 January 1860.

shouting 'Who robbed the parson's house and who stole the sheep?' This related to recent unsolved crimes in the village, but the taunts had not bothered him.

Police Sergeant Clarke testified that he had seen Giles Gaylard and his party at one o'clock shortly before the meeting with PC Marshman. The defendant had appeared very much the worse for drink and was using threatening language. The sergeant stated that Giles Gaylard was shouting – 'I should like to go and fight him for a £1000' and similar threats which the officer believed referred to him even though the defendant could not have seen him at the time. However, Sergeant Clarke went on to say that Giles Gaylard was a quiet man when sober.

Mr Jolliffe told the Bench that he would prove that the language complained of had not been used, and claimed that there was animosity between his client and PC Marshman. He believed that the policemen had 'stretched their belief for the purpose of getting him convicted of the charge. With regard to the language, it was a mere matter of supposition on the part of the police, just as much as when the sergeant thought his client's remarks were intended for him even though the officer was out of sight at the time.' The solicitor went on to say that his client had been at a wedding party at his brother's house, and he then called several witnesses to show that he was not intoxicated and did not use abusive language.

The first witness was Mrs Job Gaylard (Giles' sister-in-law), who stated that the defendant had left her house between midnight and one o'clock, he was not the worse for liquor and had only been drinking very moderately.

Next came Mrs Gould, who testified that she had been one of the party with Giles Gaylard. He had been very merry, as they all were, but he was not drunk.

Several other members of the wedding party came forward and confirmed that Giles Gaylard was not drunk but merry, and sang a song about 'the bobbies'.

The case had now been presented and the magistrates concluded that Giles Gaylard – 'was not in a state to be termed drunk' and dismissed the charge.

However, the Bench had not finished with the Gaylards for the next case involved Job Gaylard, Giles' brother, described as 'a beer house keeper', summoned for refusing to admit the police on 17 January. The *Western Flying Post* reported that 'Sergt. Clarke said he was on duty on the morning of the 17th near the defendant's house. It was about one o'clock. He saw lights and observed the defendant through the window. Heard several persons talking. He remained five or ten minutes and knocked for admission. The lights were put out, and the defendant's wife went upstairs, looked out at the window and said, "We are gone to bed." The witness replied that if he was not admitted he would report the house. There was no answer made. He heard parties moving about, and afterwards, he went to the back part of the premises and found the door open. The defendant now denied the charge *in toto*; but said that he was not himself in the house. Sergt. Clarke: I saw you in the cellar, drawing cider apparently. P.C. Solomon was also examined and the defendant was fined 10s. including costs.'

MR HARDWICKE FIGHTS BACK

Mr Charles Hardwicke, a prosperous grazier and wool company agent from Hewish, near Congresbury, had made about £450 in a good day's trading at Bristol Market on 21 October 1830 and set out for home at about six o'clock that evening carrying the cash in his pocket.

Charles Hardwicke had ridden about 5 miles when he came up behind a horseman near Newland's Hatch and wished him good night as he passed. The rider whom he did not recognise in the gloom, returned the compliment and then enquired if the grazier was travelling far. When Charles Hardwicke replied that his destination was beyond Congresbury, the stranger said that he was going the same way and would be glad of his company. The two men making small talk, rode through Congresbury and about a mile or so beyond the village began to cross a lonely stretch of countryside known as the Heath. The stranger had dropped back a little when suddenly there was a loud bang and Charles Hardwick felt a violent blow on his left shoulder. Shouting 'What was that! Good God what have you done!' he turned just in time to see a flash of light. With the same, the stranger hauled his horse around and rode off at a full gallop back along the road they had travelled. Recovering, Charles Hardwicke set out in pursuit shouting 'Stop him! Stop him!' and finally caught up with his assailant just beyond the bridge over the River Yeo at Congresbury.

As the two men galloped past a cart partly blocking the road their horses collided and fell throwing their riders to the ground. Charles Hardwick scrambled to his feet and managed to seize his attacker but as he grappled with his powerful opponent he felt a sharp pain in his left side and then, stunned by several heavy blows to his head, let go. The stranger thus released remounted, but before he could ride off the grazier had recovered sufficiently to grab the horse's bridle and hang on shouting for help despite being continually punched about the head. The sound of the struggle and the cries for help brought several local men running to the scene and when Charles Hardwicke gasped out that the rider had just shot him, they pulled the

Although described by the Taunton Courier *as 'the ferocious highwayman' Richard Hewlett was captured by his badly injured victim.*

stranger down from his horse and thus secured took him to the Ship Aground Inn at Congresbury.

The parish constable, Lukins, was called and the stranger was identified as Richard Hewlett who had once farmed at Wick St Lawrence, near Weston-super-Mare. Having been accused of horse stealing some years before, Hewlett had been given £50 by a relative to leave the country and go to America where it was thought he was still living. A search of his person revealed some pistol balls, flints and powder, a map of England and Wales, a book of roads and fairs, a pocket knife and a razor. One of the villagers recovered a lead-weighted swordstick with a bent and blooded blade from the scene of the struggle whilst another had seen Hewlett throw something into the river as he was being escorted over the bridge to the inn. A search of the river bed the following morning discovered two pistols bound together, one of which had been fired whilst the flintlock on the second had fallen. However, only the priming powder in the pan had flashed and the lead ball and sodden black gunpowder remained undischarged in the barrel. The misfire of the second pistol had no doubt saved the grazier from a serious or possibly fatal wound and was the flash of light he had seen.

The surgeon called to attend to Charles Hardwicke found that he had been shot at close range, but the pistol ball was lodged too deep in his left shoulder to be removed. Also, he had been stabbed in his left side and for over a fortnight the badly injured man lay at the Ship Aground Inn too ill to be moved. At the time of Richard Hewlett's trial six months later, the court was told that it was doubtful whether the grazier would recover the use of his left arm.

Richard Hewlett appeared before Mr Justice Park at the Somerset Spring Assizes in Taunton on 2 April 1831 and after a trial lasting seven hours, he was found guilty of the attempted murder of Mr Charles Hardwicke and sentenced to death.

The *Western Flying Post* wrote that at about twenty minutes past eleven o'clock in the morning of Wednesday 19 April at Ilchester Gaol, Richard Hewlett climbed the steps to the scaffold and after praying for a short while, the noose of the rope which would end his life was placed around his neck, the white cap pulled over his eyes and he was launched into eternity. The body remained hanging for the 'usual time', was then cut down and buried the same evening.

The motive for Richard Hewlett's attack on Charles Hardwicke was never disclosed but it might be deduced from the objects taken from him at the inn that he was embarking on a life of a highwayman but at the last moment his nerve failed him and he fled. The *Western Flying Post* revealed, however, that Hewlett had hinted to the local dissenting minister from Yeovil who had attended him in his last hours that 'there were circumstances connected with this affair which would not be divulged'.

THE ICE BROKE

Christmas Time in 1901 was very cold and frosty, and across the country, people were enjoying themselves skating on ice-covered ponds and lakes.

Chard was no exception and on Sunday 22 December local people were enjoying an afternoon's skating on the Chard Reservoir which had been a popular skating rink for many years. That same afternoon, Mrs Sarah Melhuish, from Furnham Road, took her young son and his friend Eric James, for a walk to see the frozen reservoir.

As they approached the reservoir along the Chaffcombe Road, Mrs Melhuish saw a crowd gathered to look at a motor car parked on the bridge over the Chard and Taunton branch railway line, and being curious Sarah went to see this fairly rare sight; in the meantime, the young boys ran down to the nearby reservoir. Suddenly her son was pulling at her skirts shouting that Eric had fallen through the ice and running down to the shore, Sarah was horrified to see the lad struggling in the deep freezing water.

Amongst the youngsters enjoying themselves on the ice was fifteen-years-old Lawrence Hussey, of Greenhill, Furnham Road and seeing Eric fall through the ice, he skated to the rescue. As he neared the jagged hole, he lay down and eased himself slowly towards the struggling boy. At the edge, Lawrence reached out to the youngster but as he did so the ice gave way and now he was fighting for his life crying out for help in the freezing water.

An off-duty Great Western Railway locomotive fireman Alfred Pearce was enjoying a stroll and watching the skaters when he heard the cries for help and going on to the ice lay down and began to slowly edge himself towards the hole where Lawrence was struggling to keep himself and young Eric afloat. Now Alfred was in danger as the ice began to crack under his weight but he kept going only to watch the two youngsters, overcome by cold sink slowly out of sight. The gallant would-be rescuer managed to return to the safety of the shore just as the ice completely broke under him.

The police were called and Sergeant Attwood, accompanied by Constable Phillips, were soon on the scene but during the hours which followed all efforts to recover the bodies with ladders and ropes failed. A sunken boat lying at the northern end of the reservoir was raised and bailed out but when it was launched it leaked so badly that it was considered too dangerous to use.

George Warner, a marine engineer from Victoria Avenue had now joined the recovery party and organised the construction of a large raft from ladders, wooden farm gates and barrels. At about 10 o'clock that evening, George Warner and a local man, Fred Symes, launched the raft and after fifteen minutes search with a grappling line, they brought Lawrence Hussey's body to the surface; it took another hour in the darkness to locate and recover the small corpse of Eric James.

Chard Reservoir, the scene of the two shocking drownings on 22 December 1901.

In memory of this selfless act, a drinking trough was bought by the people of Chard and set up at Millfield for the thirsty horses of the town. It bore the following inscription:

> This Drinking trough was erected by the inhabitants of CHARD in remembrance of a brave deed bravely done on 22 December 1901 when Lawrence Hussey aged 15 lost his life in an attempt to save Eric James, a drowning boy, at the reservoir near this town.

Following the tragedy, one of a number which had occurred at the reservoir over the previous few years, a public subscription was launched in January 1902 to provide improved life-saving equipment and a lifeboat at the site. During the afternoon of Thursday 19 February 1903, some 300 local people crowded the bank of the reservoir to witness the launch of a punt-shaped lifeboat named *The Rescue* which would be housed in a shed conveniently placed on a nearby field. With the tragedy of Eric James and Lawrence Hussey in mind, the life-boat could be adapted for use on the ice and the Chard Town Council accepted responsibility for maintaining the boat and the lifesaving equipment.

THE KILLING ON MIDFORD HILL

Widower Jacob Wilkins was going a-courting resplendent in his Sunday best, his pockets full of half-crowns, and proudly displaying his fine silver watch and chain. The fifty-three-year-old ostler of the Blucher Inn at Norton St Philip set out on foot from his cottage at half-past eleven on Sunday morning, 1 August 1824, to pay his addresses Mrs Mary Lovington, a widow of Bath, whom he hoped to marry.

At about 2 pm he arrived at the widow's house in the city where he enjoyed a leisurely luncheon and a pleasant afternoon in Mary's company. In the early evening the couple accompanied by two female acquaintances walked to the Cross Keys Inn on the Midford road where they drank some beer. At about 8 pm they parted and Jacob Wilkins set off on the road home to Norton St Philip.

Jacob Wilkin left his home at Norton St Philip on 1 August 1824 never to return.

As the ostler was walking down the hill towards the Fox Inn at Midford he noticed a ruddy-faced young man leaning against a gate, who called out a greeting as he passed. Following an exchange of pleasantries and, hearing that he was walking to Norton St Philip, the young man joined Jacob Wilkins saying that he would accompany him so far as Hinton Charterhouse. Arriving outside the Fox Inn, his companion suggested that they go in for a jug of beer but the invitation was declined by the ostler who declared that he had no money and so they walked on past and began to climb Midford Hill.

Later that evening at about half-past nine Samuel Huntley accompanied by Mrs Ann Deverell and her daughter Ruth left the Fox Inn and had walked about half a mile up Midford Hill towards Hinton Charterhouse when a young man wearing a dark waistcoat and light breeches, came hurrying down the hill towards them. As he passed he called out that there was a man lying in the road and he had been two hours trying to get him on his feet. Samuel Huntley and his two companions hurried up the hill and as they rounded a bend a few hundred yards further along the road they saw a man lying in the dust. It took only a cursory glance to tell them that this was not a drunk but a corpse, with its pockets turned out and a badly bruised face. Samuel recognised the dead man to be Jacob Wilkins and he ran after the young man but he had disappeared. Returning up the hill he sent his two companions to the Fox Inn for help whilst he remained guarding the corpse.

The body was taken to the inn where it was confirmed that the dead man was Jacob Wilkins and that he had been beaten and robbed.

At about 10 pm there was a hammering on the door of the Lion Inn at Odd

Down, near Bath, and when she opened it, Ann Fisher, the landlord's servant, was confronted by a distressed young man soaked in sweat, wearing a dark waistcoat and light breeches who asked for a jug of beer. As the inn was closed, Ann Fisher refused but the young man pleaded that he felt sick and very fatigued as he had been walking all day from Weymouth. Seeing how hot and tired he looked, the servant relented and, inviting him to take a seat, brought a jug of beer which the stranger consumed with apparent relish. Now refreshed the young man asked for a candle to be lit and in the wavering light Ann looked on as he tried to wind a fine silver watch; also she observed that when the bill was paid the young man had a large number of silver coins.

It did not take long for the brutal murder and robbery of Jacob Wilkins to be on everyone's lips between Bath and Norton St Philip and the search was on for the young man dressed in a dark waistcoat and light breeches. The suspect was soon identified as James Reynolds a nineteen-year-old petty thief who had only recently been discharged from the Somerset County Gaol after serving a twelve months sentence for robbery; he had also narrowly missed being convicted on the capital charge of horse-stealing due to lack of evidence.

Early on the Monday morning a young man arrived at the Carpenter's Arms in the village of South Stoke, near Bath, and offered a silver watch to be raffled. However, there were insufficient takers and finally, he sold the watch to Samuel Noele for sixteen shillings.

Mr George Fisher, a farmer of South Stoke, was told of the sale and having heard of the murder and robbery of Jacob Wilkins he became suspicious. The farmer's enquiries soon confirmed his suspicions and with the assistance of some of his labourers, the young man was seized as he sat outside the Carpenter's Arms. Despite protesting his innocence he was brought before the local magistrate, Mr Edmund Anderdon and named as James Reynolds, who also went under the alias of James Walters. The watch he had sold to Samuel Noele was identified as having belonged to Jacob Wilkins, but Reynolds swore that he had bought it for £1 from a stranger he had met on the road from Bath. He refused, however, to account for his movements during the night before he was arrested.

The magistrate spent the rest of Monday examining witnesses and on the following morning James Reynolds was committed to Ilchester Gaol to await trial at the forthcoming Assizes.

At the inquest into the death of Joseph Wilkins, the jury returned a verdict of wilful murder against James Reynolds.

Just under four weeks later on 28 August the trial of James Reynolds for the Wilful Murder of Jacob Wilkins and the stealing of a silver watch to the value of twenty shillings was held before Sir Charles Abbott at the Somerset Summer Assizes at Wells and long before the court opened at 9 am, the streets were thronged with people anxious for a glimpse of the prisoner as he was brought from Ilchester Gaol.

Mr Gunning, counsel for the prosecution outlined the case against the accused and described the events leading up to his arrest.

His first witness was George Wilkins, the son of the deceased who confirmed that when his father had left home he had been wearing the silver watch sold by the prisoner. Mrs Mary Lovington described the last afternoon she had spent with Jacob Wilkins and testified that he was wearing the silver watch when he had bidden her good evening outside the Cross Keyes Inn. Samuel Huntley recalled finding the body and identified James Reynold as the young man he had met on Midford Hill.

John Wheeler testified that the prisoner had left the Fox Inn at 7 pm on that Sunday evening and gone towards Bath but he had returned along the road between 8 pm and 9 pm in company with the deceased. The witness stated that he had overheard Jacob Wilkins decline the prisoner's invitation to have some beer saying that he had no money and recalled Reynolds saying 'Well then we will go to Hinton.'

Ann Fisher, the servant at the Red Lion recognised the prisoner as the young man who had called on the Sunday night and identified the silver watch he had tried to wind as that owned by the deceased.

William Perry told the court that the prisoner had returned to the lodgings they shared at Rush Hill, just outside Bath at about 11 pm on that Sunday night in an agitated condition. He had shown the witness a silver watch and some silver money, but would not say how he had come by the articles. Early the following morning James Reynolds had left saying he was going into the city. William Perry went on to say that he had never known the prisoner to have a watch before.

Samuel Noele testified that he had bought the silver watch from James Renolds for sixteen shillings at South Stoke on 2 August. On hearing of the murder and robbery and Mr Fisher's enquiries, he had taken the watch to the farmer.

At this moment Mr George Fisher was asked to produce the watch and the witnesses formally identified it as either belonging to the deceased or seen in the possession of the prisoner.

Mr George Goldistone, a surgeon of Bath, stated that death had been caused by a violent blow to the left side of the head which had fractured the skull. He believed that a round stick could have been used to inflict the injury.

Joshua Hunt, a police officer at the Walcot police office in Bath where James Reynolds had been taken following his arrest at South Stoke, was called and testified that when the prisoner had been in his custody he had said that no one had seen him do the deed and therefore they could not hang him for having Jacob Wilkins' watch. Before the witness could continue, the prisoner who until now had shown little emotion or interest in the proceedings suddenly shouted out, 'That's false my Lord!' but the officer insisted that he was telling the truth.

The prosecution's case was now complete and Reynolds was called upon for his defence. Protesting his innocence he swore that he had bought the silver watch from a man called Lacey and had as much right to buy it as to sell it, but then said no more.

The judge, Sir Charles Abbott summed up the evidence for the jury who took only ten minutes to find James Reynolds guilty of the Wilful Murder of Jacob Wilkins and he was sentenced to be hanged.

The condemned man was taken back to Ilchester Gaol to await his execution and there he confessed. He stated that he had met Jacob Wilkins between the Cross Keys and the Fox Inn at Midford and seeing the silver watch and chain he was determined to steal them. Having got into conversation with the ostler he had walked with him towards Hinton Charterhouse and going up Midford Hill he had picked up a stone about the size of a hen's egg. He had concealed it in his hand and about halfway up the hill he had struck Jacob Wilkins one heavy blow on the left side of his head. Jacob Wilkins had fallen down on his face and James Reynolds stated that he had taken the silver watch and some coins. He expressed great sorrow and that he only meant to stun Jacob Wilkins.

The *Western Flying Post* had reported in detail on the trial of James Reynolds and on 13 September 1824 recounted:

'That on Monday last [6 September] James Reynolds, alias Walters, underwent the sentence of the law at the drop erected in front of Ilchester Gaol, having been convicted at the last Wells Assizes of the wilful murder of Jacob Wilkins. Since his conviction, he has conducted himself in a becoming bearing and acknowledged the justice of his sentence but declared that his intention had been only to robbing the deceased. The Rev. Mr. Valentine, the chaplain to the gaol, was unremitting in his endeavours to bring him to the nature of his awful situation which he happily accomplished. The wretched culprit was attended by the Rev. Gentleman early in the morning of his execution who administered to him the Sacrament; shortly afterwards the Under-sheriff arrived and every preparation having been made, the procession moved slowly from the chapel to the lodge, the Chaplain reading aloud the first part of the Burial Service, during which the prisoner wept bitterly Having ascended the fatal platform they continued in prayer for about ten minutes; and precisely at a quarter past eleven the signal having been given, the drop fell and he was launched into eternity; he died without a struggle. His body after hanging the usual time was cut down and conveyed to the Taunton Hospital for dissection [by Mr Lyddon]. The number of spectators to view this melancholy sight were comparatively few to what have been witnessed on former occasions. Reynolds was a stout and rather good looking person, only 19 years of age, but a very depraved character. A few months only before the commission of the crime for which he suffered he was discharged from Wilton Gaol, where he had been confined twelve months for a robbery; he also confessed that in July last he attacked with his usual weapon (a stone), a butcher on his return from Melksham Fair whom he dreadfully ill-treated and left unconscious after robbing him upwards of £6.'

TRAGIC DROWNING TRAGEDIES.

Cricketsham was a popular bathing spot on the River Yeo by the railway bridge which carried the line from Yeovil Town Station to Yeovil Junction. The station now forms part of the Yeo Leisure Park, the bridge long since demolished, but the river flows slowly and slightly menacingly as it did on an August evening in 1878 when several youngsters were enjoying themselves in the cool water.

Tom Cunningham and his non-swimmer pal, John Parker, had been larking about in the shallows and as they climbed back up the bank, Tom shouted out to another boy by name of Lydiatt, that if he would swim across he would do the same. Without waiting for a response to his challenge, Tom jumped back in and struck out for the opposite bank. When he was nearly threequarters of the way across, Tom suddenly screamed for help and with a flurry of splashing water, went under.

The lad resurfaced but began to sink again. Two older boys, Robert Jennings and his friend Galliott had just finished swimming and were drying themselves on the opposite bank when they heard the screams for help. Running to the water's edge, both boys jumped in. Robert held on the abutment of the railway bridge and young Galliott holding his free hand stretched out to reach Tom before he went under again. Despite Galliott's efforts, it was too late and the youngster disappeared for the last time.

Tom Cunningham's body was recovered the next day, and the inquest jury meeting in the Crown Inn recorded death by 'Accidental drowning.' The Deputy Coroner, Dr Garland, and several members of the jury expressed regret that there were no public swimming baths in Yeovil and the doctor went on to say that he felt public swimming baths would be 'conducive to the healthiness of the place and tend to diminish the number of deaths by drowning whilst bathing in the River Yeo'.

Tom's final resting place is in Yeovil Cemetery where his headstone bears the words – 'Drowned whilst bathing – August 26th 1878'.

In 1885, the Yeovil Borough Council opened the first public swimming baths in the town.

On a warm July afternoon in 1893, the River Yeo was the scene of another tragedy involving a young boy, nine-years-old Garnet Score.

The 11th of July was a Tuesday, and just after two o'clock, Garnet left his home by Yeovil Bridge proudly carrying a new ball. His mother, Mary, watched the youngster run across the neighbouring field, closed the door and resumed her household chores.

By early evening, Garnet had not come home and his parents began to feel anxious because the lad had never been away so late before. Thinking that Garnet, might have gone to Yeovil for some unknown reason, Mary hurried into the town but her enquiries of friends and relations drew a blank; no one had seen Garnet.

By now Mary was beginning to fear the worse and went to the police station to report him missing.

With still no sign of Garnet the following morning, the Sherborne police were informed as the Score's home was on the Dorset side of the River Yeo, and together with constables from Yeovil, a search was made of the river downstream from Yeovil Bridge but there was no sign of the missing boy.

The lake at Brympton House where tragedy struck on 3 September 1878.

On the following Thursday morning, fourteen-years-old Martha Conway, who worked for the Score family, happened to be walking along the river bank when she saw what she thought was a boy's cap in the water, but to her horror, a closer inspection revealed that it was Garnet's head.

Martha ran for her life to the Score's house and broke the news. Mr Score and his neighbour Elias Bartlett, hurried to the spot and dragging Garnet's body from the river, laid it on the bank and sent for the Yeovil police,

The story which emerged at the inquest held on 14 July at Lannings Farm Cottages, told of a young boy believed to have been playing on his own near the river and somehow his new prized ball had gone into the river. Garnet had tried to retrieve it by reaching out hanging onto a clump of charlock (wild mustard), pieces of which were found clasped in one of his hands, the charlock had given way, and the boy, a non-swimmer, had fallen into the river and tragically drowned.

The police witness, PC F. H. Miller, told the inquest that there were no unusual marks on the river bank and no signs of violence on Garnet's body

The jury returned the verdict of 'Found drowned.'

The beautiful little church of St Andrew, Brympton D'Evercy, with its unusual bellcot, stands close to the equally beautiful Brympton House, one of the finest in Somerset. The name of the collection of Hamstone buildings which form this small settlement derives from the D'Evercy family who were lords of the manor in the thirteenth century and who, with their successors, lie buried in and around the church.

There are many memorials to the Clive-Ponsonby-Fane family who owned the Brympton Estate in the eighteenth, nineteenth and twentieth centuries and includes one to sixteen-years-old Eleanor Ponsonby who was drowned in the lake of Brympton House on 3 September 1878.

Laughing and chattering three young ladies ran across the terrace of Brympton House and down to the lake where the small rowing boat was moored against the bank. 'I'll row,' called out Caroline Gore as she scrambled aboard followed by sisters Margaret and Eleanor Ponsonby. Could anyone think of a better way of enjoying that early September afternoon in 1878 than a trip on the lake in the splendid surroundings of Brympton House.

We are not told whether Caroline Gore was a proficient oarswoman, but somehow the boat ran against the bank at the place where the feeder stream flowed into the lake. The girls tried to push the vessel away from the bank, but as they did so the bow dipped, and water poured over the side. The laughter turned to screams of fear as the boat rapidly filled and then capsized tipping the occupants into the lake.

John Bullen, the butler, was going about his daily duties in the House when he heard the screams, and rushing out to the terrace saw to his horror, the boat turn over and sink. He raced across the lawn, and although he could not swim, jumped into the lake and waded out to the rescue. Gardener, John Redward, had also heard the screams and came running in time to help the butler drag Caroline Gore and Margaret Ponsonby onto the bank. John Bullen then went back to help Eleanor, but although he waded out as far as he could, she was out of reach, and the gallant butler who could not swim, was almost out of his depth. There was no way he could rescue the drowning girl and was forced to return to shallower water. Alas, John Redward the gardener was also a non-swimmer, and both men watched helplessly as Eleanor disappeared into the dark waters. By now the household was rushing down to the lake, but it was too late, Eleanor Ponsonby had drowned.

The body was recovered later in the afternoon and on the morning of 4 September, the coroner held his inquest at Brympton House. Miss Margaret Ponsonby and Miss Caroline Gore gave their evidence in a private room and the jury also heard from the butler and the gardener on the unsuccessful attempt to rescue Eleanor. A verdict of 'Accidentally drowned' was returned and the jury gave their fees to the Yeovil Hospital.

Eleanor's grave is in the northeast corner of the churchyard, together with those of other members of her family, all of which lie north/south and not the usual east/west.

In the same churchyard of St Andrew's lies young Thomas Old, a glover, who ten years later went to Weymouth on Bank Holiday Monday, the 6 August 1888.

Shortly after he arrived, Thomas went down to the beach and hired a canoe. The boatman warned him not to go beyond the pier, but being a daring young fellow, Thomas paddled on and on. The captain of the yacht *Kitty*, cruising about a mile offshore, suddenly noticed someone struggling in the water and altered course to assist. On reaching the spot all he found was an empty canoe and a man's hat bobbing on the surface of the sea – of the struggling figure there was no sign. The canoe was towed ashore and the name and address of the hirer were established, Thomas Old of Brympton, near Yeovil. Six days later, Thomas Old's body was discovered by a boatman taking a fishing party to Portland. How he came to drown was never established, but it was suggested at the inquest that Thomas may have tried to stand up in the canoe and fell out because canoes could be notoriously unstable craft to the unwary. His brother told the inquest that he did not think Thomas had been out in a canoe before and was not used to boating. A verdict of 'Found drowned' was returned and the body of twenty-two-years-old Thomas Old was brought back home and buried in the quiet churchyard of St Andrew's. His epitaph reads – 'Beginning to sink he cried Lord save me. – St. Matthew xiv – 30.'

A POET A NAVIGATOR AND A DEADLY ENCOUNTER

East Coker is an attractive village and is complemented by the church of St Michael which stands to the south, next to Coker Court. A church stood on this site in Saxon times and rebuilding during the succeeding centuries has resulted in the impressive building overlooking the village at the beginning of the twenty-first century.

The ancestors of the American poet, Thomas Stearns (T.S.) Eliot left East Coker for the New World in the mid seventeenth century, and the poet returned to his English roots on several occasions before his death in 1965. On Easter Sunday in 1965, T.S. Eliot joined his South Somerset ancestors, when his ashes were buried at St Michael's church where there is a plaque in his memory bearing the first and last lines of his poem 'East Coker':

'In my beginning is my end
In my end is my beginning'

Another monument in St Michael's remembers William Dampier, explorer, buccaneer and hydrographer, who was born in Hymerford House, North Coker, in 1651; he would almost certainly have known T.S. Eliot's kin. Dampier's career was truly remarkable, he circumnavigated the world at least three times, and was the first to explore the north-west coast of Australia.

Entering the small gate on the footpath leading to the north porch, there is a headstone which reads:

In Memory of
Nathaniel Cox
a Police Constable of this
County who was killed whilst
in the discharge of his duty
on the night of November 16 1876
Aged 37
In the hour of death and in the day
of judgement, Good Lord deliver us

The killing of PC Nathaniel Cox and the serious wounding of his colleague PC Henry Stacey by suspected poachers caused uproar in the community, and the sentences handed down to the four men involved (a father and two sons from Hardington Mandeville and a man from West Coker), were very contentious. All four were charged with murder which carried the death penalty, but because the policemen were known to have had alcoholic drink on that night, and it proved

Monuments in the church of St Michael, East Coker, remember the poet T. S. Eliot and William Dampier, explorer, navigator and buccaneer, and in the churchyard, lies the body of Police Constable Cox.

impossible to establish who struck the fatal blows, the jury returned verdicts of guilty of manslaughter. Five years after that dreadful night, the case returned to public attention. However, let the following article in the *Western Gazette* of 18 November 1881 tell the story to which there is an interesting sequel:

'PC Cox of East Coker and PC Stacey, of West Coker, were on duty near Netherton, in the Parish of Closworth, on the night of the 16th November 1876, when they saw George Hutchings (an aged man), Peter Hutchings, Giles Hutchings (his sons), and Charles Baker (the finest man of the party), returning homewards through a lane with a cart which appeared to be heavily laden. Knowing the proclivities of the men, and thinking they had been on a poaching expedition, the policemen stopped the cart, whereupon they were assaulted in a savage manner with sticks, and, it was supposed, a life preserver or a hatchet. Cox was killed on the spot, and Stacey was left in a ditch in an insensible state. He, however, soon recovered consciousness and succeeded in crawling to the residence of Mr Marsh, of Darvole Farm, where assistance was procured, and the body of PC Cox taken to the New Inn, at East Coker. Baker was soon apprehended, but the Hutchingses eluded the police for several weeks – the greater part of the time, it was believed, hiding themselves in the woods in the neighbourhood, although a few days after the murder they were driven into Dorsetshire. Having been traced back to their native place, however, the various woods in the neighbourhood were "drawn," but the murderers could not be unearthed. At length it was ascertained that the three

Hutchingses had been seen at West Coker; and on Thursday, January 18, 1877, the police were fairly on their track. Deputy Chief Constable Bisgood superintended operations; and so closely was every house in the village watched, that two of the prisoners (George Hutchings and Giles Hutchings), finding that it was impossible to obtain food in their hiding place gave themselves up to Mr Vagg, a butcher, of West Coker, who on Friday morning Jan. 19th, drove them to the Police-station, at Yeovil, covered over with a tarpaulin. When taken out of the cart, they were found to be in a wretched plight from exposure. Peter Hutchings was captured by the police in Mr Vagg's stable on Saturday morning (20th) and lodged in the Yeovil Police-station. When removed from his hiding place, he appealed to the police not to hurt him. The prisoners were tried at the Somerset Assizes at Taunton, in March 1877, before Lord Chief Justice Cockburn. They were each sentenced to 24 years hard labour. After sentence had been passed, Baker made a statement to the effect that the old man didn't leave the cart; and, on the recommendation of the Judge, George Hutchings was soon liberated. He at once returned to Hardington, but he survived only a few months. Giles Hutchings escaped from Chatham Prison about twelve months after his committal, and, it was reported at the time, had been seen in Hardington, but although the police made enquiries in the neighbourhood and carefully watched his house, they were unable to find the escaped convict. It was then rumoured that he had gone to America, but many persons entertained the belief that he was drowned whilst attempting to swim across the Medway.'

The *Western Gazette* went on to report on 18 November 1881, that a man fitting Giles Hutchings' description had been found living in a small cottage outside the village of Niton on the south coast of the Isle of Wight. Despite protesting that he was not Hutchings, the man was taken into custody on suspicion of being an escaped convict, but on the way to Newport, he had made a break for freedom. After a long chase over streams and fields, the suspect was recaptured and on reaching Newport police station, the 'delicate-looking fellow, about 36 years of age, with flowing beard and bilious complexion,' was identified as Giles Hutchings from the description on the wanted posters. Formal identification was given by several warders from Chatham Prison, and Giles Hutchings was taken under close guard to Pentonville to serve out the full term of twenty-four years penal servitude. It was reported that for most of his time on the run, Giles Hutchings had adopted the name of Williams, and had lived the quiet life of a labourer raising pigs and fowls, and tending his small cottage garden. He had worked for a time as a bricklayer's labourer on the building of the new police station and cells in Newport!

THE YEOVIL SMALLPOX HOSPITAL

It is difficult to understand, in a world from which the scourge of smallpox has now been eliminated, the fear which this disease could generate. For centuries, smallpox was a fearsome and nauseating viral disease, highly infectious, and if the patient did not die in the most loathsome manner, the disfiguring scars left on the survivor could be appalling. The introduction of vaccines by the pioneering work of Edward Jenner and Yetminster farmer, Benjamin Jesty, at the end of the eighteenth century, and the subsequent refinements in the process, lessened the severity of the disease but epidemics still occurred. Smallpox was always lurking somewhere and great was the fear when the disease broke out.

The early isolation of cases of smallpox and the immediate vaccination of contacts was the main reaction of the authorities charged with the custody of public health during the nineteenth century. Many city and town councils built hospitals to isolate the deadly infectious diseases, such as scarlet fever and diphtheria, and special hospitals were provided for isolating smallpox cases. This is the story of the Yeovil Smallpox Hospital and as some of the events occurred just over a century ago, it shows the great advances which have been made in medical science and the treatment of disease.

In 1870, Yeovil suffered a serious outbreak of smallpox and although the number of cases was relatively small and there were fewer deaths compared with other fatal infections, the memory was traumatic and still lingering twenty years later. At the Yeovil Town Council meeting of 6 March 1893, the Borough Surveyor could still cause shudders when he reported 'The only matter which called for attention for February was a case of smallpox. Owing to the prompt action of the superintendent of police, the bedclothes which the patient had used during her fortnight stay in the town were destroyed within an hour of the case being notified.' The Sewage Committee followed with a report on two sites for a suggested small isolation hospital for the treatment of smallpox and cholera cases. One site, and that favoured by the committee, was in a field owned by the council at Lyde Lane some half a mile from Sherborne Road, and the other was in a field in Ilchester Road near the cemetery! The council decided to build the hospital, with accommodation for a caretaker, wife and four patients at Lyde Lane, where the nearest house and public road were over 200 yards away. At the following meeting, plans of the scheme were presented and passed, although one councillor objected to the estimated cost of £400 being charged to the rates 'as the building would to an extent be erected for the benefit of posterity'.

Despite the speed at which the council built the hospital, two years later in the summer of 1895, Dr Garland, the Medical Officer of Health, reported that it had not yet been used.

This happy state of affairs was not to last, for in the following November, the first case of smallpox was admitted to the hospital from a house in Orchard Street and, due to the prompt action of the medical officer of health and Mr Eveleigh, the sanitary inspector, the danger of an epidemic was avoided and no other cases occurred. The patient, who came from Exeter, survived the ordeal.

Trouble broke out again in March 1896 when a case of smallpox was admitted to the Yeovil Union Workhouse in Preston Road. There was no specific accommodation in the workhouse for isolating the victim who was placed in a small, smoky, low-ceilinged room, 15 yards from the dining hall and the men's and children's wards. Dr Marsh, the union's medical officer, supported by the Poor Law Guardians, made a personal plea to the council to allow the Lyde Lane hospital to be used for this patient. Although the council had a legal right to refuse admission, Dr Marsh hoped that it would 'not allow any feelings of red-tapism to interfere with their legal duty to the community and for the sake of public safety'. However, the doctor was reminded quite forcibly that when the council had asked the guardians to join in providing an isolation hospital for town and country cases they had declined to do so on the basis that they had sufficient accommodation of their own. Doctor Marsh and the poor law guardians were then lectured by the councillors over their 'petty fogging policy' and other similar matters. Although the guardians had some supporters on the council, their plea was dismissed on the grounds that, although the hospital was empty, the victim had been in and about Yeovil on market day and it might soon be needed by people he may have infected. It was suggested that the guardians might put up a temporary structure in the grounds of the workhouse for their case!

Two further smallpox cases were subsequently isolated in the town, but no more occurred at the workhouse and all three patients, one a child, survived and made a full recovery. During the next five years, there were no smallpox outbreaks and the isolation hospital slipped quietly out of the public gaze as the council concentrated their efforts on other municipal matters.

The opening years of the twentieth century were greeted by the last great epidemic of a severe form of smallpox, Variola Major. Between 1901 and 1905 some 4300 people died of the disease in Great Britain and 1902 was the worst year with over 2000 deaths. The council was now thrown into a state of near panic because in December 1901 they were informed that following a High Court decision, a local authority with an isolation hospital could be required to accept 'paupers' with infectious diseases. The council could now be forced to accept patients from the Workhouse and armed with this decision the poor law guardians refused to co-operate in providing funds to extend the four-bed Lyde Lane establishment to cater to the possible increased need. With smallpox raging in the country and a suspected case taken into the Lyde Lane hospital, the Medical Officer of Health reported to the council in January 1902, that if an outbreak of the dangerous and highly infectious scarlet fever occurred in Yeovil, there would be great difficulties in isolating these patients, many of whom would be children, as well as smallpox cases. The council was also reeling from the shock of a major collapse of some 243

The first case to be admitted to the new smallpox hospital was a young boy from Orchard Street shown here in the early 1900s.

feet of a main trunk sewer which had just been laid from the Pen Mill Sewage Works to the west of the Town Station.

What could be done? Various suggestions were put forward, including the construction of a galvanised iron shed or a tent, in the grounds of the isolation hospital or in the council's adjoining field. The council decided, however, that during the national smallpox outbreak only patients with the disease should be admitted to the hospital. Mercifully, the suspected case did not develop smallpox but the seeds of doubt about the adequacy of the isolation arrangements had been sown. The Sewage Committee were instructed to look into the matter and the following June they recommended that a mortuary and washhouse should be added to the Lyde Lane hospital which should then be used for infectious diseases other than smallpox, and a site acquired for a special smallpox establishment. Government rules prevented smallpox hospitals from being built within a quarter of a mile of any hospital or dwelling and therefore the council could not build the new smallpox hospital in the surrounding fields it owned at Lyde Lane.

In the summer of 1902 smallpox broke out in the area and the Yeovil Town Council debated long and hard on what should be done to protect the townspeople from this dread disease. Earlier thoughts about the provision of a special smallpox isolation hospital were thrust aside in the need to do something quickly and the council decided that only smallpox cases should be admitted to its general isolation hospital at Lyde Lane. It was agreed, however, to appoint a married couple as caretakers, together with a trained nurse to take charge of the hospital in the event of an outbreak of the disease because, as an alderman reminded the council 'It is necessary for a caretaker to be appointed and it is highly necessary in the interests of the trade of the town, retail and staple, to have a trained nurse when there is an infectious disease.' He seemed to have forgotten the interests of the health of his fellow townspeople!

Thankfully, Yeovil escaped the epidemic and once again the subject of a smallpox hospital slipped from council and public gaze in the shadow of more interesting topics such as the long-running battle between the council and its former borough surveyor, Mr Armytage, over fees alleged to be owed him for water and sewage works projects.

In July 1903, a serious and potentially deadly scarlet fever epidemic broke out and the Lyde Lane hospital could not cater for the large number of patients, mainly children and young people, going down with this highly infectious disease. The council discussed the possibility of purchasing, either some Berthon pre-fabricated wooden and iron-framed huts or putting up tents for the patients. It was decided to buy two Berthon huts because they could be dismantled when they were not needed and were also recommended for use in smallpox outbreaks.

During the previous months, talks had been taking place with the Yeovil Rural District Council on a scheme for building a 20-bed isolation hospital in Yeovil or near Odcombe, to be shared between the two authorities. The town council decided, however, not to enter into a joint arrangement, because now it had agreed to provide the additional hutted accommodation at the Lyde Lane site, Yeovil was self-sufficient. The need to provide a remote site for the smallpox hospital had not been entirely forgotten but it seemed that landowners were not particularly anxious to offer land to the council; one site at Marston Magna was offered for £325 but this was rejected as too expensive.

The Medical Officer of Health, Dr Garland, now put forward a claim for a salary increase arising from the greater workload he had undertaken in connection with the scarlet fever outbreak and in January 1904 the council decided to make enquiries of other towns to find out how they paid their medical officers for such work. Sadly Dr Garland died shortly after the council meeting.

During 1904, the Lyde Lane hospital was in constant use, mainly for the treatment of scarlet fever, and smallpox once again slipped from the agenda. The subject resurfaced in October 1904, when the council was offered the twenty-one-years lease of a field some 3 miles from Yeovil adjoining the present A37 Dorchester road at Whistlebridge. The Sanitary Committee prepared a scheme for siting a smallpox hospital in the field, either in the form of a temporary shed or a tent, together with a water supply and a tree planting screen along the roadside. The matter was discussed at the December meeting when a councillor voiced his concern at the proposal because he understood that the field was liable to flood and exclaimed that 'This is a nice place to put a smallpox patient in a canvas tent!' However, the council decided to proceed with the scheme and the Lease was entered into.

The site now awaited its first patient and this was not long in coming. On 17 June 1905 a case was isolated and the fifty-years-old man who had come to Yeovil from Somerton, where smallpox had broken out, was hastily isolated in one of two Berthon huts taken from the Lyde Lane hospital and quickly erected at Whistlebridge. Dr Page, the new Medical Officer of Health, reported to the Council that he believed the outbreak had been contained and the question of providing a permanent store building in the field was discussed. Dr Page suggested that the building would store the collapsible Berthon hut because they could not be properly disinfected, and he did not think it wise for them to be returned to Lyde Lane after use. There was also the problem which could arise if there were patients of both sexes at Whistlebridge as they could not share one tent or hut, and the nurse employed to look after them would have to live somewhere on the site. No action was taken on Dr Page's suggestions and the smallpox patient, who only suffered a mild attack of the disease, left his hut at Whistlebridge some fourteen days after admission.

Smallpox struck again in October 1905 when a nine-year-old boy contracted the dreaded disease. The medical officer of health reported that the case had come to his attention as he was passing the boy's home and the mother had called him in to see what was wrong with her son. It appeared that the boy had been confined to bed for one day but had been at school on the two previous days. Dr Page found the lad to have the characteristic eruptions of the fourth or fifth day of a smallpox attack, modified by primary vaccination. The two huts were quickly re-erected at Whistlebridge and the nurse and the boy were installed the same evening. Disinfection of the victim's house was carried out and all members of the patient's family were re-vaccinated. The source of the outbreak could not be traced, although it was believed that a hawker of goods, who had lodged nearby, was the probable carrier of the disease. After isolation for five weeks and a cost to the council of £15 for his treatment, the boy recovered and was sent home.

Once again Yeovil had a lucky escape because no other case occurred the town, but Dr Page once again impressed on the council the need for a permanent store at Whistlebridge in view of the considerable work which had been required to bring the site into use at short notice. He believed any delay could increase the danger to the public and having experienced the shock of two outbreaks of the disease in one year, the council finally agreed to build a galvanised iron store building on the site.

Finally, the council had established a smallpox hospital for the townspeople of Yeovil, albeit in a very rudimentary form, some twelve years after the subject was first debated. A serious outbreak occurred in 1909 when one patient died and the hospital was in use for some two months. Several months later, the Sanitary Committee reported to the council that at the time of the smallpox outbreak, Mr Abbott, the former inspector of nuisances, was supplied with a mackintosh at the council's expense for use in connection with his duties. The mackintosh was still in Mr Abbott's possession, and when the Town Clerk had asked for its return, the former employee had claimed that it had been given to him. The Sanitary Committee disagreed, and recommended that court proceedings should be taken for the recovery of the garment. A councillor wondered whether it was advisable to have the coat back after it had been used in the smallpox hospital, but there was laughter when another councillor understood that Mr Abbott wore it to his Sunday chapel meetings. The recommendation was adopted but history is silent on whether the mackintosh was recovered.

The Whistlebridge hospital was never used again after the 1909 incident and in 1922 the field was leased to a local farmer. As the century progressed, so did community action to contain all forms of infectious diseases and in 1929, Yeovil joined in a county-wide scheme to contain smallpox. The lease of the Whistlebridge field was surrendered in 1930 and because no-one wished to buy the Berthon huts they, and all other equipment, were burnt.

The Lyde Lane isolation hospital was taken out of use in the early 1930s and during World War II served as a mortuary for air raid victims and as a hostel for 'difficult' evacuee children. The building was demolished in the 1960s when the Yeovil Borough Council developed the site and surrounding land for the Pen Mill Trading Estate.

BIG BANGS

Big Bangs in Yeovil

On Saturday, 14 March 1868 there were complaints to the Manager of the Yeovil Gas Works about a strong smell of gas in Wine Street. Two workmen, Messrs Budgell and Munford, were sent to deal with the problem and on locating the possible source of the gas leak began to dig up the street. Unknown to the diggers, a sewer had been laid alongside the gas main, and suddenly Mr Budgell's spade broke into the sewer pipe. There was a massive escape of inflammable sewer gas and as Mr Budgell struck a match to see what had happened the sewer exploded, blowing out parts of the floors and yards occupied by Mr Holland, Mr Childs and Sgt Holwell and sink traps in other neighbouring houses. Fortunately, there were no casualties apart from two very surprised workmen who would no doubt exercise more caution were searching for smells.

Sixty-five years later at 5 a.m. on Saturday, 3 June 1933 many Yeovilians were rudely awoken by a loud bang; the new 18-inch gas main in South Street had exploded. Living in one of the nearby houses were Mr and Mrs Harry Robus and their nine children. 'I thought a bomb had exploded,' Mrs Robus told a *Western Gazette* reporter, 'I heard the shattering of glass and looking out of the window I saw a cloud of black and yellow smoke rising from the trench.'

On 3 June 1933, an 18-inch gas main exploded in South Street not far from the entrance shown here.

Another woman said that she had found herself on the floor and did not know whether she had been thrown out of bed or what had happened.

Mrs Peaty of 35 South Street described how her house had been shaken by the explosion and not a single pane of glass was left intact. The kitchen had been filled with soot dislodged from the chimney by the blast and her daughter, Hilda, told how she had been woken up to see flying glass and sand coming through the bedroom window.

Neighbour Mr S. Pitman of number 37 said that it was just like a bombardment.

The nearby Methodist church was untouched, but all the windows of the Boxall Works on the other side of South Street were shattered.

Thankfully no one was hurt and the damage was mainly confined to broken windows; incredibly several of the residents of houses next the explosion slept through it all!

The official statement from the Town Clerk confirmed the rumours that the main had burst during pressure testing.

By the way one of the films showing in the Palace Theatre near the site of the explosion was *Handle with Care*

Some months later, Councillor Fudge, the Chairman of the Gas Committee, informed the Borough Council that the explosion had been caused by the 'excessive zeal of one of the workmen' who had ignored the order not to proceed with pressure testing the new main until the responsible man had arrived. Councillor Fudge stated that all the insurance claims had been settled and no further action would be taken.

Big Bangs near Winsham

Victory in Europe (VE-Day) on 8 May 1945 was a celebration like no other. Across the nation there were street parties, dancing, bonfires and all sorts of jollifications, including fireworks, to celebrate the defeat of the Nazis. However, the explosive celebrations proved a little too exuberant at Closewood Farm in the hamlet of Ammerham near Winsham on the day following VE-Day, when according to the *Western Gazette* of the 18 May a local agricultural and forestry contractor 'was in the mood for jollifications and he thought he would make a small bang in the little hamlet'.

The contractor broke in half one of the sticks of Burrowite explosive which he used for removing tree stumps, inserted a detonator and a fuse into each piece, lit the fuses and threw the pieces out of the kitchen window. The resulting extremely big bangs blew out six of the farmhouse windows, left two small craters in the lawn and frightened the neighbours.

However, this was not the end of the story, because a few days later he appeared before the Chard magistrates charged with failure to hold explosive licences under the Defence Regulations, was found guilty and fined.

THE WYVERN'S DOWN!

The Wyvern was a large single-engine strike fighter designed by Westland Aircraft of Yeovil to meet the Admiralty's specification for a large carrier/land-based fighter with the capacity to operate in an anti-shipping role. It was a machine of complex design and in the autumn of 1949 was still in its development stage with all the dangers and difficulties this entailed.

Monday morning, 31 October, was a crisp autumn day under a clear blue sky when Westland's Assistant Chief Test Pilot, Squadron Leader Mike Graves, DFC, took the Wyvern prototype VP113, powered by a Python turboprop engine fitted with two contra-rotating propellers, up for a routine test flight from the company's airfield at Merryfield, near Ilminster. As it flew over Yeovil the aircraft developed engine trouble and Mike Graves made for an emergency landing at the Westland airfield. The stricken Wyvern swooped low over the town and across the airfield, climbed over Preston Plucknett and banked left for a landing approach from the west with its engine stopped. The aircraft came in wheels up for a forced 'belly' landing at something like 200 mph but despite Mike Graves' efforts to reduce the speed, it crossed the crown of the airfield before it touched down. The Wyvern bounced into the air, ploughed through the eastern perimeter fence killing little five-years-old Ann Wilkins as she pedalled her tricycle along the cinder path from Westland Road to Seaton Road, smashed on across a piece of open ground through gardens, destroying fences and outhouses, and finally crashing into 30 Westland Road. Demolishing the house, the aircraft exploded in flames, killing the pilot and Mrs Edith Brown who died instantly in the ruins of her home. The next-door house, number 28, was also in flames and trapped in the doorway between the kitchen and the living room by the collapsed rear wall was Mrs Edith Hockey surrounded by fire.

Amongst the first to arrive at the scene of devastation was Reg Holland from his shop on the corner of Orchard Street, and George Hulbert with his son Ron from their Beer Street motor workshop. Together with Messrs Warton, Govier, Williams and Moulding, they fought to free Edith Hockey from the blazing wreckage but were forced back time after time by the smoke and flames. The Westland Works firemen were quickly on the spot and soon after the town's appliances arrived, followed by foam tenders from Royal Naval Air Station, Yeovilton. Divisional Officer Charles Mitchell, commander of the Yeovil Fire Service, led the attempts to free Edith Hockey and as his men fought to keep the fire back, Station Officer Richards burrowed through the rubble to release her legs whilst Sub Officer Newman and Fireman Hardy worked from the opposite side of the debris. Station Officer Richards later recalled how he had felt a fluffy bundle, which for a moment he thought was a child, but found it was Mrs Hockey's little dog who scampered away when he freed it. Dr J.C. McMaster, who had been at Westland Works that morning, hurried to the scene and despite the horrific conditions managed to

The Westland Wyvern prototype which crashed on 31 October 1949.

administer a pain-killing morphia injection to the badly burned Edith Hockey who was finally freed after half an hour's suffering. She was rushed to Yeovil hospital but tragically died two days later. The efforts of the fire crews saved the remaining two houses in the terrace and after two hours the flames were out.

Recalling the events of the morning, Mrs Arnold of 24 Westland Road. told how she was preparing dinner for her brother and sister when the roar of the crash sent her diving for cover under her sewing machine. Recovering from the shock, she ran outside to find the area ablaze and made a futile attempt to fight the fire with buckets of water – 'It was a hopeless task,' she said. Another housewife, Mrs Hann, at 32 Westland Road told how she was preparing dinner when she heard a plane go over but took little notice as low flying aircraft were commonplace. Shortly after there was a violent explosion as the Wyvern ploughed into number 30 next door.

Part of one of the aircraft's wings, complete with fuel tank, cartwheeled over the houses and struck the home of the Mills family at 16 Westland Road. Although the wall of the house was damaged, the fuel tank did not explode, and the only occupant at the time, the Mills baby escaped unhurt; its mother having just popped out to see a neighbour.

At the inquest which followed, Westland's Chief Test Pilot, Mr Harald Penrose, described the final moments of the doomed Wyvern. He said that the flight was a routine experimental test, and when he first saw the aircraft it was flying at about three hundred feet with both propellers stopped and the undercarriage retracted. It was apparent that Sq. Ldr Graves was in great difficulty in attempting to make a forced landing on the airfield before reaching the eastern perimeter. The Wyvern was travelling at well over 200 miles per hour but when the pilot realised he would overshoot, he had made a deeper dive which must have further increased his speed. It was a gamble whether he could get down and despite everything Sq. Ldr Graves could do, Mr Penrose believed that he did not have a chance at the speed he was travelling.

A senior officer of the Accident Investigation Branch of the Ministry of Civil Aviation stated that the Wyvern's engine was stopped when it crashed but despite a thorough examination of all the components it was not possible to discover whether this had been due to fuel starvation or some other cause.

Addressing the jury, the deputy coroner stated he believed that once the pilot had realised he was in difficulties he had taken the only action he could to prevent the machine from dropping in the middle of the town with more disastrous consequences and that he must have known that he never had a chance. He thought it was a credit to test pilots that they felt it was not only their duty but their honour to try and get the aircraft down so that any cause of difficulty could be discovered.

Verdicts of Misadventure were returned on the victims and the foreman of the jury stated that 'the pilot of the aircraft did everything humanly possible to bring the aircraft down on the airfield. We consider that he had so short a time in which to do anything that he did the best he could under the circumstances and that he realised that he was going to his death.'

In all 127 Westland Wyverns were built and the aircraft finally entered squadron service with the Fleet Air Arm in 1953. Wyverns flew in the Suez Campaign in 1956, the only occasion when a British turboprop-powered aircraft saw combat and was the last conventional aircraft designed and built by Westlands Aircraft (Leonardo).

HIGHWAY ROBBERY

Travel has always had its risks, and no more so than over the rutted tracks which were the thoroughfares over 200 years ago. Not only had travellers to contend with the every-day broken wheels, axles etc of their carts and carriages, broken heads and bones from being thrown from the horses or conveyances, but there was the threat of having one's brains blown out by a thug on a horse!

At about eight o'clock on a Thursday evening in October 1777, Miss Joliffe and her friend, Miss Starke, were returning home to Crewkerne on their post-chaise after a pleasant day in Ilminster, when they were held up and robbed by 'two highwaymen, one mounted on a bay horse, near 15 hands high'.

Following this robbery, the two 'gentlemen of the road' went on to attack several other travellers on the Ilminster road that night. Almost certainly the same highwaymen carried out another robbery early in the following month and once again the victim was a lady, but, who on this occasion turned out to be a most resourceful one! The *Western Flying Post* wrote that; 'On Thursday last, Mrs. Rowsell, of Merriott, Somerset, was attacked on the road between Haselborough turnpike and the crossroad that leads into Crewkerne, by three highwaymen. The first rode up on a bay horse, and had a black handkerchief or crêpe tied over his face with a dark brown greatcoat, and asked her if she sold butter? She told him that she sold rolls, and had been to Haselborough with them, on which he presented a pistol to her and said he would blow her brains out if she did not deliver her money; on which she put her hand into her pocket, and delivered all the money that was in it, which was about thirty shillings, in silver and halfpence;

Mrs Rowsell on her way home to Merriott was robbed near Haselbury Plucknett.

after which he obliged her to turn her pocket inside out. She had slid into her bosom a guinea, and twelve shillings and sixpence in silver... The other two men that were with him were mounted on black horses and had brown great coats on.'

Following this episode, the robbers seem to have departed the area for there are no more reports of their activities.

However, not every 'gentleman of the road' remained free to carry on with the trade.

Just outside Ilchester on the western side of the A37 road to Yeovil was a field called Gallows Five Acres where, until the 'new drop' place of execution was built at Ilchester Gaol in 1811, all malefactors sentenced to be hanged met their end. David Davis, highwayman, went to his end at Gallows Five Acres in September 1778, and in April 1783, highway robber, John Wharton met his on the end of a rope followed the next day by William Lattimore, another highway thug, but this time at Taunton. In 1784 highway robbers Richard Rendall, John Jones and Thomas Phillips met their ends at Gallows Five Acres and four more of their brethren joined them the following year.

By the time Ilchester Gaol closed some fifty-eight years later, twenty highwaymen were hanged either at Gallows Five Acres or on the 'new drop'.

By 1839, when my next story takes place, railways were beginning to be laid across the country, road surfaces had improved, and on the whole, travel was becoming less hazardous, but danger still lurked for a lone traveller on a dark night.

At about six o'clock in the evening of Monday 2 December, the Reverend Champness Pleydell Bragge, left Chard and was riding home to Sadborow House, near the Dorset village of Thorncombe. He had visited his solicitors in the town and was travelling home carrying a large sum of money – £120 in £10 banknotes drawn of the Stuckey's Banking Company, some gold sovereigns and silver coins.

About a quarter of a mile outside Chard, suddenly out of the darkness, three villains rushed the reverend gentleman, dragged him off his horse, and whilst one covered his eyes and mouth the others rifled his pockets taking the notes, cash, a valuable watch and a notebook. With their haul, the thugs ran off in the direction of Chard, but not before one of them had delivered a nasty blow to the victim's head.

Recovering from the blow, the Rev. Bragge managed to secure his horse and made his way back to Chard 'considerably frightened'. The authorities acted swiftly and details of the banknotes were circulated to banking houses in the area and some suspicious strangers were arrested at the town's White Horse Inn. It was the day of Chard Great Market and of the many people who had attended the market, there were some who could be regarded as being of a 'suspicious' nature. However, following questioning by one of the local magistrates, the strangers were released.

At Bridgwater, the following day, twenty-five-years-old coal miner Thomas Stone, and Samuel Frappell, thirty-five, a butcher, both from Bedminster, were arrested following their attempts to exchange the stolen banknotes and were found to be in possession of more of the Stuckey banknotes, together with a quantity of gold and silver coins. Of the third robber, there was no sign and it seems that he had got clean away but with none of the loot.

Thomas Stone and Samuel Frappell appeared at the Somerset Assizes on 2 April 1840 and were found guilty of assaulting the Rev. C. P. Bragge 'on the highway and stealing £120 in notes and other monies' and sentenced to fifteen years transportation.

On 7 September 1840, Samuel Frappell left England on board the convict ship *Lord Lyndoch,* bound for the penal colony in Tasmania where he arrived with 320 other convicts on 4 April 1841. Thomas Stone sailed for Tasmania on 21 April 1842 in company with 299 other convicts on board the *Susan* and arrived three months later on 25 July.

SOMEWHAT SHOCKING, SURPRISING, AND STRANGE

A Shocking Death

On 9 September 1878, workmen were laying gas pipes by the South Western Railway line near Yeovil Junction. Work stopped at one o'clock for dinner, and one of the workmen, sixty-years-old labourer, Elijah Pound, decided to cross the rails to visit a hut where men working on the track sometimes took their meals. Finding it empty, he returned and began to walk beside the track to join his fellow workmen for dinner. A Great Western Railway passenger train was approaching from the Yeovil

"The Castle of Comfort."
QUANTOCK HILLS.

The ghostly horses and hearse were not seen passing the Castle of Comfort.

direction and Elijah stopped to watch it pass. However, unnoticed by the labourer, a South Western Railway engine was coming down the line from Yeovil Junction to Yeovil Town Station on the track by which he was standing. Alfred Reader, who was working nearby saw the engine and shouted to Elijah Pound to watch out! Too late, the front buffer plank which projected from the side of the engine struck the labourer's head. The unconscious man was loaded onto a trolley and taken down the line to the Town Station, from which he was conveyed to his home. Doctor Colmer was called but despite his efforts, Elijah Pound died at eight o'clock the following morning without regaining consciousness.

The *Western Gazette* reported in September 1878 that at the inquest, into the death Elijah Pound, Mr Howell, the Manager of the Yeovil Gas Works, stated that the men laying the pipes had been repeatedly told to keep watch for trains, but the deceased had been 'an obstinate man, and did not like to be spoken to about it'. The inquest jury returned a verdict of accidental death and added that no blame could be attached to anyone.

Something of a Surprise?

It might come as something of a surprise to know that during many years of the nineteenth century Martock was the venue for first-class horse racing and drew many thousands of racegoers to the village. For example, Tuesday, 18 September 1827, was a 'red-letter day' for Martock. It was the day of the MARTOCK RACES,

which attracted a large crowd of lovers of the turf and 'first sportsmen' to the course. The *Western Flying Post* recorded that:
'The Races took place on Tuesday last. From the great number of good horses that were entered, great sport was anticipated, and there were very admirable running and jockeyship. The number of persons present were computed at 25,000, among whom were some of the first sportsmen in the west of England. The weather was very favourable, and the scene altogether most enlivening. The following is a correct account of the running:-
The Martock Stakes, a sweepstake of 19 Sovereigns each, with 40 Sovereigns each:-
    Mr. White's b. g. *Pavilion*... 1
    Mr. Chambers's br. g. *Gas Light* ... ...2 dr.
    Mr. Richards's b. g. *Habberley* ... ...3 dr.
    Mr. Westbrook's br. m. *Lottery*... ... ... dis.

These heats were admirably contested, and won by only half a head. The Stewards' Cup:-
    Mr. Chambers's br. g. *Gas Light* 1
    Mr. Symes' br. m.*Governess*, late *Virgin*... 2
    Mr. Slade's br. m *Polly Hopkins*... 3
    Mr. White's bl. m. *Gipsey* 4
    Mr. Westbrook's br. m *Lottery* 5
    Mr. Alexander's br. f. *Little Jane* 6
    Mr. Hewett's b. g. *Ranger* ... ... dis.

The Hunters' Stakes of 5 Sovereigns each with 40 Sovereigns added.
Five horses were entered for these Stakes, but were not in a condition to start after the hard running for the Stewards' Cup.

A Handicap of 5 Sovereigns each with a Purse added for the beaten horses; heats twice round:-
    Mr. Westbrook's br. m *Lottery* 1
    Mr. Symes' br. m. *Governess*... 2
    A good race: won by half a head.'

Something Strange

In the 1850s, a Miss Williams of Over Stowey had a frightening experience which was recounted by C.H.Sp.P. in the 1891 edition of the *Somerset and Dorset Notes and Queries*:
'Miss Williams of Over Stowey, was returning home from Watchet late in the evening when her pony fell and hurt its knees so badly that she was obliged to walk. After proceeding some distance finding it was growing dark, and being 7

or 8 miles from home, she engaged a young man at Putsam to accompany her. It soon became very dark and as they were passing through a thick wood and the ground was very wet, and she felt very tired, she again mounted the pony. They had not gone far thus, when she found her pony become very restive, trembling exceedingly, and trying to push sideways through the hedge as it to avoid something. Every effort to make him go on was useless. After a while, a crashing sound was heard, lasting only a second or two (a kind of clatter like the trucks in Bristol loaded with iron rods). After a few minutes the noise was repeated, still more loudly. The pony now was ungovernable and Miss W. was obliged to ask the man to hold him by the head. On being asked what was the noise the man seemed much frightened. And said that he had never heard anything like it. The noise was repeated a third time and which such an overwhelming crash, that Miss. W felt unable to bear it and stopped her ears. The man was perfectly overpowered with alarm, and sunk to the earth in an agony of fear. Miss W. then observed something approaching which passed close by her, having the appearance of a hearse drawn by four horses, but no one with them and not the slightest sound. On Miss W. asking the man what he had seen, he described exactly the same. After this, they neither heard or saw anything and the pony went on freely, indeed seemed to hurry homewards. In about half a mile they came to the public house called the 'Castle of Comfort' where several men were sitting outside the house smoking. Miss W. asked if they had seen anything pass. They said they had not, though they had been sitting there more than an hour and there was no other way through the wood. They reached Over Stowey about 11, and the young man declared that nothing should induce him to pass through the wood again at night, so he remained till morning. The story soon got wind, and some of the older people of the neighbourhood 'wondered how Miss W. could venture to pass through the wood at night', it was so noted for extraordinary noises, &, ever since a dreadful murder of a woman by her husband, who was hung on a gibbet near the spot.'

The place of Miss William's ghostly encounter was almost certainly Walford's Gibbet, not far from Over Stowey, where John Walford was executed for the murder of his wife in 1789.

THE BATTLE OF LANGPORT

The reasons for the years of turmoil between 1642 and 1646 which afflicted the British Isles, and which we know as the Civil War between King Charles I and the Parliament, are many and complex. Suffice to say that the effects of the Civil War were shocking for tens of thousands of people throughout the country, and the good people of Somerset suffered from the ravages of sieges, rampaging soldiery, famine and plague, or in the words of a contemporary commentator:

'The whole country was in confusion and distress. Much land lay untilled. Farmhouses were often plundered and sometimes deserted and burned. Wounded soldiers, disabled from further service, begged on the highways. Deserters from both armies ill-treated travellers, searched wagons, forced themselves upon wives and families whose husbands were absent at the war, lived at free quarters upon the helpless, robbed the hen roosts and sometimes taken in the act were recognised by former comrades and speedily hanged.'

The Civil War broke out at the beginning of August 1642 and the Marquis of Hertford was sent into Somerset by King Charles I to raise forces for the Crown. At the same time, local supporters of Parliament had been raising their army and before long a clash between the opposing forces would be inevitable. One of the first skirmishes of the Civil War took place at Marshall's Elm near Street and the Royalists were the victors.

Nearly three years later in July 1645, when the Civil War was finely poised, one decisive victory or defeat could decide the conflict and change the course of the of these islands' history. Although King Charles I had been heavily defeated during the previous month by the Parliamentary New Model Army at the Battle of Naseby, the Royalists were still in the field, and the King, who had retreated to Hereford, now looked to the West Country where there was still hope for his cause

A photograph taken in 2018 looking towards the New Model Army's position from the Royalists' lines on Ham Down.

General Lord George Goring and his Royalist army were in Somerset besieging Taunton, the only important Parliamentary garrison left in the West of England. If Taunton fell, and Goring could bring his army to join the King, the Royalists would become a force to be reckoned with, and this might encourage Parliament to seek peace.

The Parliamentary leaders were aware of the danger and also were looking west. Sir Thomas Fairfax and Oliver Cromwell, were despatched with the New Model Army to destroy the Royalist army; a kingdom was at stake.

Learning of the approach of the Parliamentary army from Dorset, Goring broke off the siege of Taunton and marched south to defend the line of the River Yeo and Parrett from Langport to Yeovil and the three river crossings. The New Model Army entered Crewkerne on Saturday 5 July and reconnaissance parties reported that the Royalists were concentrating at Langport, the bridges at Long Load and Ilchester were defended and the bridge at Yeovil broken down.

On 7 July, the New Model Army assembled between Crewkerne and Merriott, and Fairfax and Cromwell, with a large escort, carried out a reconnaissance of the country towards Long Load. Finding the Load Bridge heavily defended and receiving a report that Yeovil was not garrisoned, Fairfax marched his army in a swift manoeuvre to the town and the broken bridge was put under repair. The Royalist garrison at Ilchester, recognising that the seizure of the river crossing at Yeovil exposed their left flank, abandoned the town and fell back on the main army at Langport.

The New Model Army occupied Ilchester on 8 July, and Fairfax received intelligence that Goring had withdrawn his garrison from the Load Bridge and was also moving from Langport to march on Taunton, possibly with the intention of one final assault to take the town and establish his own garrison. The Parliamentary position could then be critical because the Royalists could be reinforced from Wales and Ireland through the Somerset ports controlled from Taunton.

However, the move towards Taunton of a large body of cavalry commanded by Lieutenant General John Porter was a feint to draw the Parliamentarians in this direction, whilst Goring withdrew the main army to the Royalist stronghold at Bridgwater.

To hinder the Royalists' move, Fairfax ordered Major General Massey with some 4500 men to intercept Porter, and on 9 July Massey surprised the Royalists, who believing that the New Model Army was miles away, were relaxing in the meadows of Islemoor. In the fight which followed over 500 Royalists were captured but the majority escaped back to Langport.

Whilst this action was underway at Islemoor, Fairfax and the rest of the New Model Army marched from Ilchester to Long Sutton. The detachment of Major General Massey had depleted the main army and even with reinforcements drawn from the Yeovil and Crewkerne areas, Fairfax had no more than 8000 men, roughly the same size as Goring's force.

THE BATTLE OF LANGPORT

Scouts were reporting that the Royalists had not vacated Langport and appeared to have every intention of standing and fighting. However, what the Parliamentary commanders did not know, was that Goring had decided to withdraw to the strong Royalist garrison at Bridgwater and during the night of 9/10 July most of the cannon and the baggage wagons were despatched.

Early in the morning of 10 July, the New Model Army marched out towards Langport and at about seven o'clock formed up east of the town on the ridge of Pitney Hill facing Ham Down. The Parliamentary army comprised seven regiments of horse together with musketeers and pikemen. Following a Council of War, Fairfax decided to attack, even though his army would have to force its way across a difficult piece of country and into a fortified town With the arrival of the New Model Army, the alarms were sounded in the Royalists positions and Goring, deciding that he could not complete his withdrawal, marched his men out to form up on Ham Down.

Between the two armies lay a valley, through which ran (and still does) a stream called the Wagg Rhyne with marshy ground on both sides and which could seriously hamper an advance by either side in extended order. However, there was one way through. A narrow lane, now the Langport to Somerton road, crossed the valley and over the stream through a deep muddy ford. Goring quickly despatched a strong force of about 3000 musketeers to defend the hedgerows on the slopes of Ham Down and cover both sides of the ford. As most of the Royalist artillery was now on the way to Bridgwater, Goring was acutely short of cannon and placed the only two guns he had retained at the top of the lane to fire down its length and sweep the ford. The Royalist cavalry was assembled on the crest of Ham Down supported by infantry.

Fairfax and his cavalry commander Oliver Cromwell surveyed the enemy strong positions, and they could observe that the hedges of the enclosures on the slopes of Ham Down, and around the ford, were lined by several thousand musketeers. The Parliamentarians would have to advance down the slope of Pitney Hill and cross the stream, whilst the only approach firm enough for the heavy cavalry would be through the ford and up the narrow lane before they could deploy to the Royalist front. The lane was scarcely wide enough for four horses abreast and with musketeers lining the hedges on both sides, together with the cavalry and the two cannon at the top, this would be a hazardous undertaking.

Fairfax, however, had the advantage of more heavy cannon, and the battle commenced with a ferocious barrage laid down on the Royalist position. The cannonade was so heavy and accurate, that Goring's two guns were quickly put out of action and he was unable to reinforce his infantry manning the hedgerows commanding the ford. Under the cover of the cannonade, Fairfax sent forward a division of 1500 musketeers under Colonel Rainsborough to clear the hedgerows to enable the cavalry and infantry to cross the Wagg Rhyne. The Royalists did not give ground easily, but they were finally driven from the hedgerows around the ford and the crossing was won. The Parliamentary cavalry could now advance to form upon the enemy side, but this manoeuvre was not without hazard. The horsemen had to cross the deep muddy ford, move up the narrow lane, and then deploy to the enemy's front. During this time there was the great risk that Goring's cavalry would charge down and destroy them piecemeal as they came out of the lane. Only highly trained troopers could attempt such a manoeuvre, commanded by the boldest of leaders. Cromwell, for once, did not lead his cavalry in person, which perhaps indicates the danger of the enterprise, but ordered one of his bravest officers, Major Bethel, to lead the assault

Major Bethel charged through the ford and up the lane, but with only half his men deployed, the situation became dangerous when over 400 enemy cavalry moved down towards them. Although outnumbered, Bethel and his troopers charged the Royalists with such fury that their front rank was thrown into disorder. More Parliamentary troopers were coming out of the lane and the fighting became a general melee. Despite being still outnumbered, Bethel's men held their ground and Major Desborough's troopers, who were now over the Wagg Rhyne, launched themselves at the Royalist flank. Desborough's assault demoralised Goring's cavalrymen and at this moment Colonel Rainsborough's musketeers poured a withering fire into the Royalist infantry and drove them back up Ham Down. The front ranks fell back on the reserves, order was lost and the cavalry fled through their supporting infantry. Panic is infectious and within moments the Royal army turned and ran, several regiments without firing a shot.

The greater part of the defeated cavalry retreated for the shelter of the stronghold at Bridgwater by way of Aller, where a rearguard action was fought against the pursuing Parliamentary horse, but the majority kept going and did not draw rein until they reached the walls of Bridgwater. The surviving infantry and some cavalry fled as a body through Langport, down Bow Street, which they set fire to cover their retreat, and over the bridge seeking to reach Bridgwater along the left bank of the River Parrett. Oliver Cromwell led the pursuit through the flames sweeping across Bow Street, over the bridge and captured several hundred Royalists at Stathe.

The Langport Fight, as it was known, and the rout of the last Royalist army of substance is said to have sealed the fate of King Charles I. Although the English Civil War dragged on into the following year, 1646, the King could never muster an army in England sufficient to threaten or defeat the Parliamentarians. The New Model Army had proved itself at Naseby and again at Langport, and was now unstoppable.

The war came to an end when the main Royalist stronghold of Oxford fell in June 1646, by which time King Charles had surrendered to the Scots and on a cold January day in 1649, he would lose his head on the scaffold outside Whitehall Palace in London.

CAR THIEVES

In the early hours of 7 May 1919, one minute wholesale fruiterers, Messrs Parson & Co's nearly new American Hupmobile touring motor car was parked at London's Covent Garden Market, and next, it was gone. The description of the alleged thief which fitted that of a known malefactor, namely Vivian Rupert Blackmore, was circulated immediately to police forces around the country, and later the same morning, a man answering the description of the said Vivian Rupert Blackmore was arrested in Dorchester following the sale of the Hupmobile to local garage proprietor, Mr Ford. However, Vivian Rupert Blackmore was either a very resourceful individual or the Dorset police were somewhat careless because on his way to the police station he escaped from custody and disappeared

Once again Blackmore's description was circulated to police stations and on its receipt at Yeovil, the owners of local garages, pubs and hotels were quickly notified. At about ten o'clock on the following morning, the Yeovil police received a telephone message from Messrs Hill and Boll, The Garage, Kingston, stating that a customer fitting the description of the wanted man was in their showrooms asking to hire a car to drive to Basingstoke.

Police Sergeant Valentine was dispatched on his bicycle to Kingston and on entering Messrs Hill and Boll's showrooms, a man answering Blackmore's

Vivian Rupert Blackmore was arrested in Messrs. Hill and Boll's showrooms on Kingston.

description made a bolt to leave. However, the sergeant was too quick and detained the man informing him that he was suspected of stealing the Hupmobile at Covent Garden Market and that he was taking him into custody. Vivian Rupert Blackmore did not resist and replied 'Yes, that is so.' Sergeant Valentine then searched his prisoner and found banknotes and cash amounting to £308 17s 2d, a small fortune in 1919 values.

Vivian Rupert Blackmore went quietly to Yeovil police station to await the arrival of Metropolitan police officers to escort him on his return trip to London.

Four months later on 26 September, the following headline grabbed the attention of readers of the *Western Gazette* – 'MOTOR THIEVES IN THE WEST'.

On Thursday morning, 18 September, three young men called at the Brunswick Street premises of Yeovil motor car proprietor, Mr T. Heard, and made arrangements to be driven to Weymouth. However, at the appointed time only two turned up and told Mr Heard's son, who would be driving them, that their friend would be late and asked if they could sit and wait for him in the car, a new Ford. This Mr Heard junior readily agreed, as it would give him time to grab some lunch before they set out and so he went back indoors leaving the two men sitting in the car, one of whom had taken the front passenger seat.

The sound of the car's engine interrupted Mr Heard junior's lunch, but by the time he reached his front door, the Ford and its two occupants were at the end of Brunswick Street and turning left onto Hendford

The Yeovil police were quickly informed and a description of the Ford, registration number Y5131, was telephoned to police stations in the area. Reports began to come in that the Ford had been seen passing through Crewkerne and Chard going west on the Exeter road, and following receipt of the message at Honiton, PC Champion was sent to patrol on foot the main road through the town. There were few cars on the road and the top of the High Street, PC Champion flagged down the first motorist coming from the Chard direction. In reply to the officer's enquiry, the driver recalled passing a car answering the description of the stolen Ford and almost immediately the wanted vehicle and its occupants appeared. PC Champion, rather foolishly as it turned out, stepped out on to the High Street and raised his hand for the driver to stop. Naturally, the driver was loath to obey and accelerated, forcing the constable to leap for his life out of the road. However, PC Champion was made of pretty firm stuff, commandeered the car he had stopped, and no doubt shouting 'Follow that car' or something similar, set off in pursuit. As it turned out the Ford was the faster of the two cars and soon disappeared in the distance. PC Champion, seeing a car coming from the Exeter direction, flagged it down but the driver confirmed that he had not seen the Ford. Realising that furthering the chase would be futile, he thanked the driver for his help and returned to Honiton in the commandeered car.

The stolen Ford and its two occupants were not seen again on the Exeter road and seemed to have vanished into the surrounding countryside.

However, during the following morning, the stolen car was found parked down a back road near Honiton, undamaged but with the registration number changed to Y53. Reporting on the attempted robbery, the *Western Gazette* suggested that 'The men in the car had apparently turned off the main road and had doubled back, realising that the pursuit was becoming a bit too warm. No trace of the men has been discovered.'

And finally, for car thieves, a form of justice could be swift in one part of the United States, as the following article in the *Nottingham Evening Post* of 17 June 1905 relates 'The reason for lynching a horse thief is that in sparsely settled countries, a man is so helpless without his horse that he may perish, and often does. So the horse-thief is incidentally a murderer. The Colorado Cowboys' Association, whose secretary reports that 58 lynchings occurred under its auspices in 1904, all conducted in an orderly manner, has (says *Motoring Illustrated*) passed a resolution inflicting the death penalty on motor-car thieves on the ground that a motor-car occupies the same relation to a man as his horse.'

ALIAS BLUE JEMMY

Fifty-two-years-old James Clase, alias 'Blue Jemmy' the name by which he was best known and which I will use in this tale, had a reputation as a horse thief and despite his claims to have stolen over a hundred horses, he bore a charmed life and had never been found guilty in a court of law for his depredations. Blue Jemmy had managed to stay one step ahead of the gallows; horse theft could be a hanging offence, or if he was 'lucky', a one-way trip on a convict ship to Australia.

He had, however, come pretty near to one of those fates in the spring of 1825 when he appeared before Judge Sir James Park at the Somerset Spring Assizes charged with stealing a mare from Stratton in Cornwall. Dame Fortune smiled once more when it was proven that the horse's hoofs were not all white as testified by the principal prosecution witness because one was partly black. The case collapsed and Blue Jemmy was freed to resume his 'trading activities'.

Early on the morning of Monday 10 October 1826, Mr Holcombe of Fitzhead, near Taunton, was shocked to find that his valuable bay mare was missing and was most certainly stolen as the only gate to the field was still shut. Handbills describing the mare and offering a reward were quickly distributed far and wide, and the hunt was on.

However, Blue Jemmy had been recognised the day before sitting by the road near Fitzhead and because of his reputation, he became the prime suspect.

Late on that Monday afternoon, a man rode into the yard of the Crown and Anchor pub at Mosterton leading a bay mare and announcing that he was travelling to Bridport fair took a room for the night. Landlord Mills thought he recognised the customer as Blue Jemmy and his suspicions were aroused that all was not above board when on enquiring whether the mare was for sale, the landlord was offered the bay for £18 when he knew it to be worth more than £25.

Before Blue Jemmy left the following morning, and just in case his suspicions were justified, Landlord Mills went to the stables and cut three notches in the mare's mane

On Wednesday 11 October one of Mr Holcombe's handbills was dropped in at the Crown and Anchor and from the description of the stolen horse, the landlord recognised it as the bay mare in the possession of Blue Jemmy. The local authorities were notified and a couple of days later he was caught with the stolen mare at Tiverton. Mr Holcombe identified his bay and Landlord Mills confirmed that the three notches in the mane had been cut by him at the Crown and Anchor.

At the Somerset Assizes in Taunton on 7 April 1827, charged with the capital offence of stealing the bay mare and hearing that he would be appearing once more before Judge Sir James Park, Blue Jemmy exclaimed, 'Then I am sure to be hanged.'

And this is precisely what happened. Blue Jemmy, or to give him his birth name James Clase, was found guilty and despite falling on his knees earnestly begging for his life, he was led away to await his fate at Ilchester Gaol.

ALIAS BLUE JEMMY

'Blue Jemmy' was hanged on the 'New Drop' at Ilchester Gaol on 25 April 1827.

On Wednesday 25 April 1827 on the 'new drop' at Ilchester, Blue Jemmy was launched into eternity in company with William Hewlett who was hanged for stealing seven ewes and eight lambs.

The *Taunton Courier* reporting the events of 25 April wrote that 'It is said that Clase had been brought to the bar nineteen times and had been tried at Dorchester, Exeter and Taunton.' Also, he had claimed to have stolen over 100 horses.

AVIATION THRILLS AND SPILLS

Today travelling by air is almost an everyday experience, and for some, even a boring one. However, during the early years of flying, it could be a far from safe occupation, as was painfully discovered by a pilot and his passenger at Westland's airfield on a Thursday afternoon in April 1919.

Lieutenant Bennett, piloting a Westland-built DH 9 bi-plane, and accompanied by a passenger, Lieutenant A. Ewens, of the Somerset Light Infantry attached to the Royal Air Force, took off from the airfield in the early afternoon, but over Lufton, the engine began to misfire, and the pilot turned back. When the engine cut out completely, the lieutenant put the aircraft into a glide but landed just short of the airfield on some allotments in Bunford Lane. The landing wheels immediately sank into the soft allotment soil and the machine turned a somersault landing on its back with the pilot and passenger trapped underneath. Mercifully the aircraft did not catch fire, and Lieutenant Bennett managed to crawl out unhurt, but Lieutenant Ewens remained trapped. Help was quickly on hand and the unfortunate passenger was extracted from the wrecked machine, suffering severe bruising and shock. After receiving first aid on the spot, Lieutenant Ewens was conveyed home to his parents' house on Penn Hill to recover from his ordeal.

An aircraft sitting on an airfield minding its own business could also suffer the indignity of being written off! Some six years later, in August 1925, Mr R. A. Bruce, Westland's Joint Managing Director, was flown in the company's Westland Limousine, to Netheravon airfield, in Wiltshire, for a business meeting. On landing, the pilot, Major Lawrence Openshaw, taxied the machine to a 'safe'

Westland's airfield in 1926.

space on the airfield, Mr Bruce went to his meeting and the major to the Mess for a rest. However, shortly after the two men left their aircraft, a flight of RAF Fairey Fawn single-engine two-seater bi-planes was taking off in line abreast, when the outer machine collided with the Westland Limousine, destroying much of the fuselage and tearing off one of the wings. The RAF aircraft was completely wrecked, but miraculously, both the pilot and his observer escaped unhurt. The Westland machine was damaged beyond repair and scrapped.

A novelty which thrilled on Sunday 7 February 1926 was a parachute drop and which was graphically reported in the *Western Gazette*:

'Yeovil people in crowds witnessed a parachute descent on the Westland Aerodrome on Sunday afternoon. The descent was made from a height of 600 feet by Captain A.F. Muir, of the Surrey Flying Services. Coming from an "Avro" aeroplane, piloted by Flying Officer E.F. Smith, he dropped 200 feet before the parachute, a "Guardian Angel," opened out. The remaining 400 feet he came down with every appearance of ease, waving his hand cheerily to the spectators and landing in full view in front of them. It was a perfectly judged feat and had the added interest that Captain Muir was performing it for the first time. Although it is demonstrated at most of the towns visited by Surrey Services, it is usually performed by Mr A.A. Anderson, who last year made as many as six descents in one week. In a demonstration of trick flying immediately after Captain Muir's descent, Mr Anderson and Mr B. Powell walked to the tips of the planes while the machine was circling in mid-air. The machines were very largely patronised for pleasure trips throughout their visit, and towards the end of Sunday afternoon had to refuse bookings. They left on Tuesday.'

However, some residents were not thrilled by the Sunday afternoon's entertainment. There were complaints about the noise of aero engines interrupting several church and chapel Divine services, and Mr Anderson expressed regret that any annoyance or inconvenience had been caused. 'We took steps this Sunday to cut out flying until the services were over,' he told a *Western Gazette* representative. 'I should like to point out however, that from the national point of view our service is a valuable reserve at no expense to the taxpayer, it keeps pilots and mechanics in training. We are not subsidised in any way by the Government.'

Despite Mr Anderson's apology, the annual meeting of the Yeovil and District Preachers' Council passed a resolution unanimously deploring the fact that a flying exhibition had been given in the town on a Sunday, and expressing the hope that those responsible would do all in their power to prevent any future exhibition of this kind on Sundays.

AND IT WAS ALL FOR A KISS

Mrs Sarah Fouraker, the wife of an Exeter police inspector, had departed the city by train on her way to Frome, in the late afternoon of Thursday 13 August 1857, and at 11 o'clock that evening had changed trains at the newly opened Yeovil Pen Mill Station. Following the stop at Bruton, the train was steaming at full speed when Sarah Fouraker was surprised to see in the dim carriage light, a man standing outside on the carriage step and looking in. She was even more surprised when he opened the door and stepped into the compartment and asked her if she wanted company as she was all alone. What happened next was recounted two days later at an inquest in the Nicoll Arms at Frome.

Miles Handy testified that he was the fireman of the Great Western Railway engine 'Leopold', which was the second of two locomotives hauling the Weymouth to Chippenham passenger train on 13 August. Driving the 'Leopold' was George Taylor, and between Bruton and Frome, Taylor had told the witness to take over the engine so that he could go back to the tender to check whether there was sufficient water to complete the journey. The next thing to happen was the guard standing on the tender shouting that the driver had fallen off and to stop the train. Miles Handy had shut off the steam, whistled to the driver of the front engine to stop and the train was reversed back to where George Taylor found lying by the track. The semi-conscious driver was lifted into one of the compartments and taken on to Frome.

The guard, Frederick Somers, stated that when the train was about a mile from Witham, he had seen the driver fall from the tender near Bull's Bridge. He had blown his whistle and at great risk had made his way along the carriage steps to the tender and warned the fireman.

Mrs Sarah Fouraker told the inquest that she had been travelling alone when the man, she now identified as George Taylor, had entered the compartment and despite her protests said that he would keep her company and asked for a kiss. When she refused the man then wanted to shake hands which she also refused. He then went back towards the carriage door as if to leave but kept returning and asking to shake hands. However, when she disclosed that her husband was a police inspector and she would report him, Taylor seemed 'very much frightened' and had quickly left the compartment.

On reaching Frome Station, George Taylor had been taken to the Nicoll Arms, where despite all the efforts of Dr White, a local general practitioner, the driver expired from multiple injuries.

The jury returned a verdict of 'Accidental Death' on George Taylor, who left a widow and two small children.

The *Somerset and Wilts Journal* in commenting on the event suggested that 'There ought to be some more speedy and effectual means of communicating between the driver and guard. The present system calls loudly for legislative interference, the

Near this spot in the evening of 13 August 1857 the driver fell from the 'Leopold' railway engine and was fatally injured.

Directors seeming blind to all that relates to the comfort and safety of travellers. Had there been, as in America, an entrance at the end of each carriage, with a public walkthrough to the tender, the present unhappy accident, by which a widow and two small children have to lament the death of their only support would never have occurred. In this instance the guard was obliged at the risk of his life, to get from the carriages to the tender while the train was going at the rate of forty miles per hour. We are informed that the usual expedient to the Great Western Railway for alarming the driver is to put on the brakes, but in this instance, there was only one guard in charge of the train.'

CRAZY RIDES

The following report was published in the *Western Flying Post* on 19 September 1865:

'At the Taunton Police Court, a case was heard in which a fearful railway adventure was brought to light involving the narrow escape of the night mail train on the Bristol and Exeter Railway. William Stevens, cleaner of railway engines was charged with wilfully causing damage to an engine to the extent of £100. The Chard and Taunton Railway is in the course of construction and is so far completed that engines can run over the rails. The duty of the defendant was to clean the engine called the "Busy Bee" every evening after the work of the day, and a half past three on the following morning to light the fire so that steam could be got up by six o'clock and the labour of the day commenced. On no account was he to meddle with the machinery or attempt to move the train, the driver laying the fire and

Privates Howes and Parks lost control of the invalid chair they were riding down Hendford Hill in July 1917.

filling the boiler with a sufficient quantity of water. The cleaner, however, took a singular freak into his head and determined to have a midnight ride. Accordingly, at midnight he lit the fire of the engine, got up steam and started the engine, he being the only passenger. Up and down the line he drove for two hours and not knowing how to precisely compress the steam it flew off in all directions shrieking fearfully and alarming the residents living close to the line. The watchman on one of the bridges was sorely affrighted at seeing an engine tearing madly along the line with a white face upon it and came to the conclusion in the darkness of the night that a ghost or the evil one himself had obtained the mastery over the iron horse. In one of his excursions, the fellow was about to enter the main line of the Bristol and Exeter Railway but he fortunately heard the approach of the night mail from London. A moment or two earlier and consequences could have been fearful to contemplate At length tired of his ride he took "Busy Bee" back to her station and laid down by the side of it to await the arrival of the driver. At half past five the driver approached the scene but when 100 yards from it the engine blew up with a fearful explosion, the cleaner having neglected to put more water into the boiler. The most remarkable part of the story had yet to be told. The cleaner although close to the engine was uninjured owing to lying down. He certainly was frightened, the driver asserted that when he came up to him his hair stood on end "like quills on a fearful porcupine". For his foolish freak he was sentenced to a month's hard labour.'

Fifty years later on a bright sunny July morning in 1917, Private Howes, late of the 20th Battalion, The London Regiment, having recovered at the Yeovil Red Cross Military Hospital from injuries received on the Western Front, pushed his pal Private Parks, 10th Yorkshire Regiment, in a Bath invalid chair up Hendford Hill, but rather than pushing him back down, Private Howes decided it would be a good idea to sit on the front of the vehicle and ride it down using his feet as brakes. This Private Howes did, but despite his frantic efforts to slow the Bath chair it gathered speed, and down the Hill they went out of control. At the bottom, the chair turned over, throwing both men out and according to the *Western Gazette* 'The men were picked up and taken into Messrs Bradford's nearby office and a telephone message sent to the Hospital. Mrs Stobart, the Commandant, despatched a nurse with another chair but in the meantime, the men were taken to the hospital in a private car. Parks was little the worse for the experience beyond a shaking. Howes sustained a compound fracture of the upper arm in the identical place that he had received a similar injury last October and for which he was brought to England.'

The *Gazette* went on to report that Private Howes had been booked to leave a few days later for a convalescent camp, but this would now be delayed. Provided there were no complications, the longer stay in the hospital might be welcomed as it would postpone his return to France. The record is silent on the future of the two soldiers but let's hope they survived the war and that neither got into too much trouble over the escapade.

FIRE AT DUNSTER

On 12 August 1818, fourteen-years-old Betty Nicholls went on trial before Mr Justice Park at the Somerset Assizes in Wells, charged with three counts of setting fire to property, including a linhay, owned by Thomas Thorn at Dunster. If found guilty, Betty would hang, or at best, be transported to Australia for life or a very long time if the Judge was merciful; arson was a capital offence. Standing in the dock with the girl was a young man called Martin Wynne, charged as an accessory before the fact in abetting Betty Nicholls in committing the crimes. Both pleaded Not Guilty. By way of explanation, a linhay, was a double-storeyed open-sided building comprising a cattle or cart shed on the ground floor, with a hayloft above, most commonly found in southwest England.

Prosecuting counsel, Mr Adams, read the first indictment, and his colleague, Mr Serjeant Pell outlined the case. He stated that on 7 January 1818, the house called Little Linhay and owned by a farmer, Mr Thomas Thorn, caught fire. The prisoner, Betty Nicholls, had been a servant of the farmer and had lived in his household for some five or six years. Martin Wynne had also lived with the family as a farm servant for nearly a year but had left service about two years before. He had then occupied a cottage owned by Thomas Thorn, but the farmer had now turned him out.

On Sunday 11 January last, Thomas Thorn and his family had left for church at about a quarter to eleven o'clock leaving Betty Nichols, servant Martha Wedlake, and the farmer's mother-in-law in the farmhouse. Mr Serjeant Pell stated that Thomas Thorn had been called from church and told that there was a fire at the farm. On arriving home he had found the Pond Court linhay next to his house and its contents of hay ablaze and a total loss; the farmhouse was also damaged. During the subsequent enquiries, Betty Nicholls said that she had seen a man, whom she did not know, come out of the Pond Court and go away down the Long Meadow.

Serjeant Pell called his first witness, the servant Martha Wedlake, who recalled Mr Thorn and his family going to church. Before her master had left for church, Martin Wynne had come to the house and stayed with Betty Nicholls in the back kitchen. Sometime after 11 o'clock, Betty Nicholls had gone out to kill a turkey for the Sunday meal, and which she brought back some five or six minutes later. The girl had plucked the turkey, and then put it on the dresser asking the witness to finish preparing the bird as she had found one of the pigs was missing and was going to look for it. Martha Wedlake stated that Betty Nicholls had gone out the front door, leaving it open, and the witness had stayed in the kitchen reading. She could not recall where Martin Wynne had gone. About a quarter-of-an-hour later, the servant stated that she had seen smoke and going out into the yard, saw Betty Nicholls looking at the hay burning in the Pound Court linhay.

The next witness, Eliza Thorn, the farmer's wife, recollected that Wynne had come to the house early on that Sunday morning to settle up what he owed on

FIRE AT DUNSTER

quitting her husband's service. He had left, but then came back at about 10 o'clock, to rectify a mistake. Eliza Thorn also stated that none of the pigs was missing because she had noticed they were all in the higher orchard when the family had left for church.

Jane Thorn, the eight-years-old farmer's daughter, followed her mother into the witness box. Despite her tender years, the court was satisfied with 'her competence to receive an oath'. The child stated that she remembered the Sunday when the linhay was on fire. She told how she had been standing in the passage outside the back kitchen, the door of which was partly open, and saw Wynne drinking a pint of cider with Betty Nicholls. Little Jane remembered him saying to Betty Nicholls 'Mind and do what I told you to do.'

A boy called Thomas Phillips, of Lower Marsh, now took the stand. He stated that at about 10 o'clock on that Sunday morning, he had walked a little way with Martin Wynne, and had mentioned two recent fires at Mr Thorn's farm. The prisoner Wynne had replied that the linhay 'would be on fire the next'.

Witness Thomas Lovell, recalled working with Martin Wynne on 4 January and was talking about Mr Thorn. Wynne had told how the farmer had accused

This photograph of Dunster at the end of the nineteenth century shows a village little changed since the case of arson in 1818.

him of stealing his turnips, and stated angrily that 'He would be damned if he would be a match for Thomas Thorn before it was long.'

Dunster innkeeper, John Strong, recollected Martin Wynne coming into his house on the day of the fire. When he said that he wondered what rascal it was who had set Mr Thorn's house on fire, the prisoner had replied that he did not know, but 'Thank God, he was hedging with Thomas Dunn – for as Mr Thorn and he had angry words, he might have thought something of him.'

Another witness, George Green, said that he had seen Wynne on that Monday afternoon, and they had talked about the fire. The prisoner had commented that he had been looking all day for them to come and apprehend him.

The Constable of the Hundred, William Little, testified that at about seven o'clock on that Monday evening, he had gone into the George Inn and Martin Wynne was one of the customers. The constable recalled that when the prisoner saw him he began to shake and denied that he had anything to do with the fire. William Little stated that he had said nothing about the fire, and in fact he had not suspected Wynne.

Witness, William Hole recalled seeing Martin Wynne in the courtyard of the farm after the fire had broken out.

The last witness, Ann Pope, another servant of Thomas Thorn, remembered Betty Nichols saying on the Sunday morning, just before the family went to church, 'Suppose the house should catch fire – It would be fun to see the people tumbling out of church one over the other.' Ann Pope had exclaimed in reply 'God forbid it should happen. One would think you had a fire in it!'

When the last witness left the stand, prosecuting counsel, Mr Adams, stated that he had offered all the evidence he had to establish the charge. However, he was anxious to have the Judge's opinion on whether Betty Nicholls' confession could be presented. This had been obtained after she had been examined by the magistrates, and after Thomas Thorn had threatened to tie her to the leg of the table if she did not confess the truth about the fire. Mr Justice Park replied that the confession could not be received in evidence, because it had been made under duress after Betty Nicholls had denied the charges under oath before the magistrates.

Following the Judge's summing up, the Jury found Betty Nichols and Martin Wynne Not Guilty.

However, there were two more charges of arson against Betty Nicholls, to which she pleaded Not Guilty, and the court proceeded to deal with the first indictment. The prosecution submitted that on 9 January 1818, Betty Nicholls was seen by three witnesses, going towards the hayloft of Thomas Thorn's upper linhay, with her hands under her apron, and when she came back her hands were no longer concealed, and the hay was on fire. An old tin pot which was usually hung up outside the farmhouse was found near the spot where the fire had started. It was alleged that she had carried some burning material in the pot to start the fire.

The jury, however, acquitted Betty Nicholls, as they believed she had no malice towards her master, Thomas Thorn.

The second charge accused Betty Nicholls of setting fire to Thomas Thorn's premises two days before on 7 January 1818, but when the prosecution declined to call any evidence in support of the indictment, the case was dismissed.

Mr Justice Park now turned his stern attention to the small fourteen-years-old servant standing below him in the dock. The Judge stated that now he was no longer prevented by law, he would say that without doubt Betty Nicholls was guilty of having committed the three serious offences. Her own confession, which could not in point of law be used against her, proved hers was the hand that committed the wicked deeds. Mr Justice Park then turned his full attention to Martin Wynne, and observed that there was every reason to believe that he had from 'some malice, or other, been an abettor in these shocking transactions'.

Betty Nicholls was taken weeping from the dock, and two very lucky young people disappeared from record.

THE PORT FOR YEOVIL

The following little story appeared in the *Western Chronicle* on Friday 5 May 1922:

'A PLEASANT EASTER HOLIDAY IN SOMERSET
By a Yeovilian

'A reader sends us an interesting account of a holiday spent this Easter on the River Yeo:

'He writes: Your readers may be interested in the account of a day spent on the River Yeo on Easter Saturday by a party consisting of three Yeovil boys, ages from 14 to 16, and myself. The boys had themselves constructed during a previous holiday, with much skill and perseverance, two small boats – one a canoe for a single person and the other a boat to seat three. Both these craft were made of hazel rods covered with canvas and made to be propelled by paddles. Last August many pleasant hours were passed in the boat at Mudford Mill Stream, but this year for the Easter vacation, a more ambitious voyage was planned, this being nothing less than a trip to Burnham, or at least to Bridgwater. So on Saturday morning we embarked at Long Load being the nearest deep water "port." This place should be of interest as only a few years ago, in the memory of many now living, it was the nearest port to Yeovil and all our coal, timber, skins and other goods were brought to this spot on river barges. Previous to the Great Western Railway coming here this now almost desolate and forsaken village was a thriving little port, doing considerable business all the year round. We made a fine start, with flags flying, and a crowd of villagers on the bridge to see us off, the mothers of the boys anxiously watching from a motor-car and no doubt wondering iif their sons would be seen alive again.

'The sun was now shining brilliantly and everything looked promising for our 25 mile voyage down stream. We could see on our right only a short distance away the beautiful church and tower at Long Load and near by the charming old Quaker Meeting House so closely associated with the Palmer family of Reading. All went well for the first two miles when our smaller craft became "unseaworthy" and its occupant thought it safe to join us in the bigger boat. We towed the other but very soon it turned turtle and eventually we hauled it on to the bank and left it there. The wind had now become a furious gale and it was increasingly difficult to make any progress. We were blown around a bend of the river at a fine speed only to find the wind dead against us as we round the corner. The first stop was planned to be at Langport, five miles down, but it took us over four hours to get there. When in sight of Mulchelney, with its church and Abbey ruins the wind and current became simply unendurable. Just here the Parrett joins forces with the Yeo and here our rudder broke, causing a leak in the stern. We had therefore to tow our poor ship another mile to Langport. We were now in quite a deplorable state, being entirely exhausted by our long fight with wind and tide, wet to the skin, our clothes plastered from head to toes with mud and slime. However, our good friends Mr. and Mrs. Richards entertained us, and after a good wash, and warm by the kitchen stove, we sat down to a well-deserved tea and soon felt restored to our usual cheerfulness. The town of Langport was then inspected, we took snapshots of the fine joint stone in the churchyard erected to the memory of the most celebrated townsman, Walter Bagehot (essayist and author of works of the English constitution). Leaving our boat to be repaired we tramped on to Burrough Bridge, a distance of some five miles, passing King Alfred's monument and wishing he had left a few of his burnt cakes for us to enjoy. At Burrough Bridge our friends at the village manse had expected us at four and had been miles up the river with ropes, hooks, etc., to rescue us from a watery grave. However "better late than never," and we spent a most enjoyable evening in the manse parlour with the piano making a fearful din in our attempt to sing every comic song we knew of. The kind Pastor and family slept on the floor and gave up their feather beds for us, so we were well rested when on Sunday we walked the nine miles to Bridgwater. This ended a most enjoyable holiday spent in our own immediate district, in our home-made boats. We recommend your readers to try the same sort of thing.'

It might come as a surprise to read in the attempt to sail down the Rivers Yeo and Parrett to Bridgwater when it was written that the village of Load Load was considered to be 'Yeovil's Port'. Interestingly back in June 1936 'An Old Yeovilian' reminisced in the columns of the *Western Gazette* on the time when Long Load was 'Yeovil's Port' and wrote of the time before the coming of the railway to Yeovil in 1853:

'A leading glove manufacturer once told me that many years ago, in 1851, the year of the Great Exhibition in Hyde Park, he took a sample case of Yeovil gloves to be displayed and to reach London by the quickest route he had first to drive the five miles over to Stoke, where he embarked on the stage-coach at Cart Gate Inn, the journey to London occupying the greater part of two whole days.

'Our general facilities for trading were also extremely limited for want of good means of transport. Unlike many towns, Yeovil had no river navigation at its door. The River Yeo was, however, at that time tidal up to the bridge at Long Load, a place some nine miles from the town, and in fact, just 83 years ago this was "the Port of Yeovil" connecting the town by water transport with Bridgwater and the Bristol Channel ports.

'The village of Long Load has always had a strong appeal for me; some of my earliest associations are linked with it. As a small boy on one visit I remember a bathe in its river and coming ashore to my horror finding my limbs covered all over with live leeches intent on reducing my blood pressure.

'The village of Long Load today is a quiet and uninspiring place, and not being on a 'bus route is seldom visited. Its one street is about a mile in length, and descends to the river, where the bridge is a natural boundary to the village. Along this street are several substantial farmhouses, but there are no other buildings of any importance. Even the church is a modern structure. Once a year the village puts on a festive appearance, this being the day of the annual fête, which is known as Long Load Revel. At the time this article refers to, Load Bridge was a place of much commercial activity. It is difficult to realise that only 83 years ago these same farm lands were the centre of flourishing business establishments. Over the bridge away from the village were the extensive stone-works belonging to a Mr Lovibond, and it is interesting to find that this gentleman's descendants afterwards developed the large and successful breweries at Salisbury and Greenwich, which reminds us that many big city firms can trace there origin to some small village industry.

'Facing Lovibond's yard on the village side of the river were the business premises occupied by the well-known firm of merchants, Messrs Stuckey and Bagehot, whose head office was at Langport. Where today only the peaceful farm fields are seen, then the ground was covered by a group of buildings, offices, weighbridge, timber shed, corn and salt stores, with stacks of bricks, pipes, slates, and other builders' materials. My connection with this firm is a family one, as my grandfather was in service of the Company for nearly seventy years as manager at Load Bridge, and afterwards at Yeovil, to which the firm moved their business when the railway was opened.

'From this near relative of mine I often heard tales of the old times at Load Bridge. He would relate to me how at certain times on the arrival of the coal boats, as many as five hundred waggons were to be seen lined up the long village street, waiting all through the night for their turn to load up at the wharf. What a lively scene this must have been, with the stamping of horses, the jingling of harness, barking of dogs and shouting of men and boys as they crowded round the yard gates at their impatience at the delay and their anxiety to get to get their loads completed and start on their homeward journey. Goods were brought up the river in large barges, some taking as much as 30 tons weight. These were towed up on the tide being drawn by specially-trained horses. In the course of the journey along the narrow towpath, at frequent intervals were stiles separating the various fields, and the barge men taught their horses to jump these obstacles – no small achievement on the part of these hard-working animals and it must have been a sight to witness.

'The river was used for a large variety of merchandise, most of which was transfered to the barges from large coasting vessels at Bridgwater. Large quantities of Dean Forest coal were handled regularly, known as Bullo coal, named after Bullo Pill, the port from which it was shipped. Culm, a kind of anthracite, came over from Swansea, and was in much demand for the numerous lime-kilns then so much in use. Salt from Droitwich, both for domestic and farm use, was another article often imported. Slates came from Port Maddoc and timber from Sweden. Bricks, tiles, pipes, and the famous scouring bricks, all were products of the Bridgwater brick fields. Chemicals and tanning materials from Bristol were brought along for the Yeovil skin yards. Soda ash for the sail markers of Crewkerne and general groceries and provisions were sent by the large Bristol warehouses. On the return journey the barges would load up farm produce, hay, straw, corn etc. for which there was a big demand for the traders at Cardiff and Bristol. Your readers will be surprised to hear that places as distant as Shaftesbury, Gillingham, Mere and Wincanton frequently made use of Load Bridge as their port, and nearer towns like Martock, Yeovil, Sherborne and Crewkerne depended almost entirely upon it for their daily supplies.'

The wharves of the port were on the right side of the image.

DEATH RODE THE SKIMMINGTON

One of the forms of rough justice handed out in the past was called the Skimmington, Skimmington Riding, Riding the Stang, Rough Music, and many other variations of the same.

The skimmington, and its many names and physical forms, was used to publicly embarrass, punish, or generally make foolish, individuals whose behaviour had caused some offence or upset, real or imaginary, to their local community or neighbours.

In 1834, the author of a *History of Lyme Regis* wrote that 'Skimmington Riding makes people laugh, but the parties for whom they "ride" never lose the ridicule and disgrace to which it attaches.'

On the north wall of the Great Hall of Montacute House, there is an early seventeenth-century plasterwork panel which depicts a hen-pecked husband having a quick drink of ale whilst he looks after the baby. On returning home, his wife is not amused and beats her husband, but this is witnessed by a neighbour who tells the village. The husband is then depicted riding the skimmington on a pole and being paraded around the village to the jeers of his neighbours.

The skimmington sometimes took the form of men and youths parading in front of an 'offender's' house and making 'rough music' by beating kettles, trays cans and buckets and anything else which could make a loud noise. Although generally harmless, the resulting stigma could lead to a family or individual moving away and on at least one occasion the skimmington proved fatal.

It was during a quiet spring evening in April 1871 when the peace of the village of Shepton Montague was shattered by the beating of kettles, old tin trays and other assorted hardware and the shouts of a score of young men as they started up a 'rough band' outside old Kitty Shears' cottage in Higher Shepton. Backwards and forwards they marched shouting that the skimmington was riding for Betty Beach, Kitty's married daughter who with her labourer husband John and their four children, lived with the old widow. Betty Beach had committed the ultimate 'sin' of usurping the male role when she stopped two boys from fighting and had given one of them a good hiding; in Shepton Montague, and no doubt in may other villages across the land, women did not 'wear the breeches' and give boys other than their own a beating. The skimmington was riding to put the matter right and Betty Beach in her place.

The cottage door flew open and in the gathering dusk, the frail figure of seventy-eight-years-old Kitty Shears could be seen silhouetted in the lamplight of the parlour.

'Be off, go away, what do'ee want making thik noise,' shouted the old lady to cheers and louder beating of the rough band which continued unabated. In her anger and frustration, Kitty shuffled to the wall of her front garden and picking up some loose stones threw them at the jeering mob.

Kitty Shears was buried in the churchyard of St Peter's, Shepton Montague on 19 April 1871.

Suddenly the old lady cried out and fell forward against the wall and began to groan pitifully before she recovered and staggered back into her cottage and the door was slammed shut. The 'band' suddenly fell silent and when someone shouted, 'She be bad hurt!', it melted away.

Kitty was indeed 'bad hurt' and fatally so, for early the next morning 15 April 1871, the widow died. The local police made immediate enquiries and her next-door neighbour, twenty-four-years-old Henry Trim was taken into custody on suspicion of throwing a stone at Kitty and killing her.

Katherine (Katurah) Shears was buried in the churchyard of St Peter's, Shepton Montague on 19 April 1871, the day on which the coroner, Dr Wybrants, held his inquest into her death. The first witness was Edwin Brown, an apprentice harness maker from nearby Bruton, who testified that on the evening of Friday 14 April between eight and nine o'clock, he had been one of a crowd watching the skimmington. He saw the old lady come out of her cottage and shout at the crowd to go away and throw the stones at the 'band' which was standing some 30 feet away on the opposite side of the road. The witness then told how he had seen Henry Trim put down the kettle he had been beating, pick up a large stone and throw it at Kitty Shears with such force that he had heard a loud thud when it hit her chest. Brown stated that he had seen no other stones thrown at the old lady. He further testified that when the crowd broke up, Henry Trim knowing that the witness had seen him throw the stone, suggested that he had been mistaken and that someone else was the culprit.

SOMERSET SHOCKING, SURPRISING AND STRANGE

The next witness, blacksmith John Hobbs, corroborated Edwin Brown's testimony.

Dr Edmund Heginbotham, of Bruton, told the jury that he had carried out a post mortem examination of the deceased and stated that in his opinion the injury to her chest caused by the stone was sufficient to cause death.

The jury returned a verdict of manslaughter against Henry Trim and he was committed to Shepton Mallet Gaol to await trial at the Wells Summer Assizes.

On Friday 3 August 1871, Henry Trim appeared before Mr Justice Willes charged with the manslaughter of Katherine Shears at Shepton Montague. When asked how he pleaded, Trim replied that he did not know whether he was guilty or not because others were throwing stones and he never saw the old woman. The prosecution was led by Mr Hooper but before he could open the case, the judge was told that the prisoner's solicitor had not given his brief to Mr Saunders, the defence counsel. However, Mr Justice Willes saw no reason for a delay and instructed the case to proceed.

The prosecution outlined the events of the evening of 14 April and Mr Hooper called Edwin Brown to recount his evidence given at the inquest. However, under cross-examination by Mr Saunders, Brown retracted the part of his evidence in which he had stated that he had seen the prisoner deliberately throw the stone at Kitty Shears. The witness now stated that he had not seen the stone hit the old lady and Henry Trim had thrown the stone with no particular aim. When asked by the judge whether this statement had appeared on the depositions, Mr Hooper confirmed that it had not, and Mr Justice Willes suggested that in the light of these new circumstances the prosecution might consider whether to continue with the case as the death would seem to be accidental. Following the judge's remarks, Mr Hooper stated that the prosecution would not press the case any further.

Mr Justice Willes then turned to the jury and said that without doubt this was a deplorable accident, stones had been thrown but the witness Brown had testified that the stone which had caused the death of the old woman had been thrown without aim or malice. Although the jury could continue with the case, the judge believed that after the admission of the witness Brown, it would be useless to endeavour to convict on the evidence now before them. The prisoner had been in gaol for three months and he considered this to have been sufficient punishment for accidentally causing the death of Katherine Shears.

Following a short consultation, the jury found the prisoner not guilty and following a caution from Mr Justice Willes against throwing stones in future, no doubt a very relieved and perhaps somewhat wiser Henry Trim went home to his wife, Martha, and young son in Shepton Montague.

However, two questions remain unanswered, why did Edwin Brown change his evidence and where was John Hobbs who had corroborated it at the inquest? Did they fear that the skimmington might ride for them?

AT RANDOM

Buying a Bird at East Lydford
From the *Western Flying Post*, 3 January 1868:
'A few mornings since. There arrived at the inn door the cart of the butcher on his weekly round, accompanied by a neighbouring farmer, with his double-barrel on his shoulder. A few knowing ones were there, doing the morning glass of bitter. After an exchange of compliments, Mr Butcher observed, "My friend here made a lucky shot on his way here, which seems rather cumbersome by the look of his pocket. Come sir, let us see the contents." "Can't do that – got no game certificate," was the answer. "What say ye," says the butcher to the farmer, "if we four each put sixpence, and have a raffle for the bird." "No objection," said the farmer, "to give it up, when you have handed over the cash, and the winner has pledged himself not to inform who killed the bird." One of the party, just arrived from the Highlands said, "Although I have not seen the bird, I should like to feel the weight before throwing in my sixpence." This he was allowed to do, and he pronounced the bird to be heavy and warm. All agreed to the raffle – one throw each. Butcher wins and now for the secret! The pocket is emptied and out comes – what think ye! Neither partridge, grouse nor pheasant – nothing but an old black rook!'

The Long Gun of Yenworthy
From *The Somerset Year Book*, 1932.
'A bare mile from the Devon border, in a hollow in the precipitous hillside overlooking the Severn Sea, stands the lone farm of Yenworthy made famous, like many other places in the district, by Blackmore, in "Lorna Doone." Here is preserved an interesting relic, a six-foot-six duck gun, which hangs upon the age-blackened rafters in the huge stone-flagged kitchen. With this ancient weapon according to tradition, a lone widow defended her home against a marauding party of Doones who attacked the farm one winter's night.

'The story as told in the book relates how the Doones commenced by firing the ricks, then "they approached the house to get the people's goods, and to enjoy their terror. The master of the farm was lately dead and had left inside the clock-case, loaded, the great long gun wherewith he had used to sport at ducks and geese on the shore. Now Widow Fisher took out this gun, and not caring much what became of her (for she had loved her husband dearly) she laid it upon the window-sill which looked upon the rick-yard, and she backed up the butt with a chest of oak drawers, and she opened the window a little back, and let the muzzle on the slope. Presently five or six young Doones came dancing a reel (as their manner was), betwixt her and the flaming rick, upon which she pulled the trigger with all the force of her thumb, and a quarter-pound of duck-shot went out with a blaze on the dancers. You may suppose what their dancing was, and their reeling now

Mr E. French shows the Long Gun of Yenworthy.

changed to staggering, and their music none of the sweetest. One of them fell into the rick and was burned and buried in a ditch the next day, but the others were set upon their horses and carried home on a "path of 'blood."

An Echo of the Klondike Gold Rush

Just inside the gate to the churchyard of St Andrew's church at Dowlish Wake and on the left-hand side stands a headstone which reads:

>Sacred to the memory of
>Ludwig Pettersen
>Pioneer of the Klondike 1898
>Born in Bergen, Norway
>1868

AT RANDOM

Died at Taunton May 22nd 1934
Aged 65
A noble minded, courageous man

Gold was discovered in Rabbit Creek in the Yukon Territory of northwest Canada in 1896 and heralded the Klondike Gold Rush, which would become one of the wildest in history. Tens of thousands of men and women swarmed into the area by steamboats up the River Yukon, or on foot over the White Pass described as the worst 'this side of Hell.' In summer the Pass was raw rock, and in winter the blizzards swept down with such fury that the Cheechakos or Tenderfoots, as the gold hunters were known, could lean against the wind and not fall over as they climbed in temperatures of -50F. During the spring of 1898, many of the Tenderfoots died when an avalanche in the Pass buried them under 30 feet of snow and rock, but they still kept coming, driven by the madness of gold fever.

By 1900, however, the gold was running out, and most of the Tenderfoots had left the Yukon for strikes in Alaska; the Klondike Gold Rush was over.

One of the tens of thousands who sought their fortunes in the goldfields was a young Norwegian, Ludwig Pettersen, who struggled up the White Pass and almost died in the terrible spring avalanche of '98. The work of digging out the dead was said to have greatly affected Ludwig, but his iron will and courage had helped him through the ordeal. Ludwig was also a friend of the author and poet, Robert Service, who wrote extensively about the gold rush, and whose poem 'The Ballad of Dan McGrew' (and its variants) is probably better known than his novels – *The Trail of '98* and *Songs of a Sourdough* – both of which were best sellers in the early 1900s.

After leaving the Klondike, Ludwig Pettersen travelled to many parts of the world before finally settling down in 1921 to carry on a poultry business in Dowlish Wake and marry local girl Kate Churchill. A local newspaper report of his funeral said that he was a man of iron will and courage, but seldom talked about his experiences.

Beware of the Scam

From the *Western Flying Post*, November 1857.

'At this season of the year, provincial newspapers are usually inundated with advertisements from pretended London salesmen, wanting supplies of poultry, game, etc. As in almost every instance the parties advertising are worthless persons, too much caution cannot be shown by our country friends in parting with their property. We have refused insertion to several advertisements, as they were evidently of a fraudulent character, but it should be understood that that the fact of an advertisement appearing in a respectable paper is not always a guarantee of its bona fide character.'

MR EDGINTON'S MISTAKE

On a Monday in late September 1901, the early evening train from Weymouth came to a halt at the home signal some two hundred yards from Pen Mill Station and waited for the Durston train to enter the station. It was 7.15 p.m. and the train on the branch line from Yeovil Town Station was over ten minutes late.

The sixth carriage of the Weymouth train was stationary on the bridge which crosses the stream from the weir pool below Wyndham Hill and, in one of the compartments, Mr Henry Edginton, a commercial traveller for the Booths Distillery Company, was dozing after a hard day's selling. Sharing the compartment with Mr Edginton, were Mr Percy Martin, the gardener at Hendford Manor and another commercial traveller, Mr Tom Lewis, both of whom were somewhat surprised when Mr Edginton suddenly stood up and opened the carriage door. Tom Lewis shouted a warning that the train was not yet in the station but, after retorting that 'I know Yeovil better than you do!' Mr Edginton, without a look, stepped out into the gathering dusk on to the parapet of the bridge and dropped some 20 feet into the stream below. The two passengers left in the compartment stared at each other in horror and on hearing a loud splash, Tom Lewis exclaimed, 'He's done for!'

At that moment the train moved forward into Pen Mill Station, and the alarm was raised. Mr Alfred Daniels, the district inspector based at the station, grabbed an oil lamp and followed by the station master, lineman Woodley and a passenger, set out along the track to the bridge. Clambering down the embankment they found Mr Edginton lying on some large stones in the shallow stream groaning and muttering, 'Where am I? and, 'I wonder what brought me here?' Nearby his undamaged silk top hat was floating in the stream. Mr Edginton was a large man, weighing nearly sixteen stones, and it took some time and effort to drag him from the stream and up the embankment to the railway track. A stretcher was sent for and the commercial traveller was carried back to the station.

Mr Edginton was placed in one of the compartments of the eight o'clock Durston train and conveyed to Yeovil Town Station from which he was gently carried to the waiting horse bus and taken to the town hospital. At about 8.30 p.m. Doctor Kingston arrived at the hospital and examined the patient whom he found to be a large, well-developed man, soaking wet, and suffering from acute shock, a large jagged cut on the back of the head and a fractured left shoulder. Despite all his efforts, Dr Kingston could not save the unfortunate Mr Edginton, who died some forty minutes later.

The inquest was held at the Victoria Hall in South Street, and after hearing the evidence from the witnesses, the coroner concluded that Mr Edginton knew Yeovil well, he had not appeared to be under the influence of alcohol, and his reason for getting out on the bridge was a matter of speculation. The coroner commented that 'There must have been a strong motive passing through the deceased's mind to get

MR EDGINTON'S MISTAKE

After retorting 'I know Yeovil better than you do!' Mr Edginton stepped out onto the parapet of the bridge and dropped 25 feet into the stream below. (The safety railings are a later addition.)

out at this place where he thought he could safely alight and felt it his bounden duty to do so.'

The jury returned a verdict of death from misadventure, and the late Mr Henry Edginton was taken home to Weston-super-Mare. The old saying 'Look before you leap' could not have been more relevant than on that September evening in 1901!

A SHOCKING AUTUMN STORM

Captain George Cope, of the ketch *Emma* did not like the look of the weather as he beat down the Bristol Channel bound for Highbridge with a cargo of coal late on Tuesday afternoon 1 October 1895. The *Emma* had sailed from Lydney earlier that day in company with the Gloucester ketch *Hereford*, Captain Thomas Guy master, also carrying coal to Highbridge. In Walton Bay off Clevedon, with the wind beginning to blow hard from the south, Captain Cope hailed the *Hereford* and announced to Captain Guy that he would make for Cardiff roads to ride out the weather rather than continue to Highbridge. The two ships parted company at about six o'clock, and the *Hereford* continued on her way to catch the early morning tide into Highbridge wharf.

Heavy waves like these at Clevedon, battered the Somerset coast during the fierce October Storm of 1895.

Although the wind was strong from the south all that Tuesday evening, there was little to indicate that it would be more than an autumn 'blow', and perhaps Captain Cope's fears would be groundless; also no storm signals had been raised along the north Somerset coast. However, by about ten o'clock the southerly wind became squally, at midnight it calmed, and then it roared out of the north-west with a violence described as the heaviest storm experienced on the Somerset coast for many a year. The storm reached its raging height between two and three on the Wednesday morning when according to the *Bridgwater Mercury*, it blew with the force of a hurricane.

In Bridgwater Bay, a number of ships were waiting to catch the flood tide to take them into the mouth of the River Parrett, and up the river to Highbridge or Bridgwater. Running before the storm, the ketch *Eliza* of Cardiff, making for Highbridge with a cargo of coal and the coal ketch *Providence*, destination Bridgwater, were in the channel of the River Parrett off Burnham, with their sails blown away. The strong flood tide raised and powered by the storm, swept the two vessels out of control up the river until they smashed into one another. So severe was the collision, both ketches began to sink under their crews who managed to escape into the *Providence*'s undamaged ship's boat and reach the shore below Highbridge Pill without loss.

At about half-past eight on Tuesday evening, Captain Crossman, master of the screw steamer *Tender* bound for Bridgwater with 150 tons of Welsh coal, brought his vessel to rest on the mud north of Steart Island to await the flood tide which would take the small ship up the river. Just after two o'clock, with the storm increasing in fury, the *Tender* with full steam up floated off the mud, but suddenly the stern swung and was caught in the mud. The steamer heeled over onto her starboard side and into the raging surf. With giant waves breaking over the stricken vessel and sweeping her deck, the mate, Henry Hawkes, and the fireman, Frederick Dennison, managed to launch and clamber into the waterlogged ship's boat. Despite their frantic efforts to reach the master and engineer, the small boat was carried away in the savage current and deposited its terrified cargo on the beach above Highbridge Pill.

Back on the *Tender*, Captain Crossman and the engineer, George Harding, were clinging to the bridge with the huge seas pushing the ship further and further onto her starboard side. With no hope of rescue in the black of the storm-tossed night, and with the stricken steamer filling rapidly with water, Captain Crossman put on a lifebuoy, shouted to the engineer to grab a plank or ladder to save himself, and jumped overboard. For nearly an hour he was swept up the River Parrett, but despite passing several ships at anchor, he could not attract attention in the howling dark. However, more dead than alive, Captain Crossman was finally rescued by the crew of the *Princess May*; of George Harding, the engineer, there was no sign.

The steamer *Bulldog*, en-route to Cardiff from Bridgwater, had anchored off Burnham, but at the height of the storm her anchor chain broke and she was driven onto the Berrow Flats. Fortunately, the vessel was not overwhelmed by the huge surf, and her crew scrambled ashore at daybreak. The *Bulldog* was refloated several days later and taken to Cardiff to be overhauled. The pleasure yacht *White Wings* moored by Burnham Pier foundered in the storm without loss of life, and several fishing boats were damaged and their gear washed away.

The sloop *Tom* of Watchet was carrying stone from East Quantoxhead to Minehead, and at the time the storm broke was anchored off Minehead waiting for the tide. As the wind increased in fury, the anchor began to drag and the sloop was being blown back across Blue Anchor Bay. Off Dunster beach, the crew slipped the anchor, set a small sail, and ran for the shore as it would have been impossible to beach the vessel near Watchet. As the *Tom* grounded the crew launched the ship's boat and with great difficulty landed on the beach. Despite their efforts, the crew could not haul the sloop above the high water mark, and abandoning their efforts for the night walked home to Watchet. At daylight, the men returned expecting to find the *Tom* smashed to pieces in the surf, but the sloop had disappeared without a trace!

George Clapp, the Burnham pilot, had a narrow escape in the storm. In company with William Howe, he had set out in the pilot boat *Halloa* to a vessel called the *Jinks* waiting in the bay. The pilot later recalled that 'There was scarcely any wind when we left the pier, and we had got about half-way out from where we had seen the previous evening the vessel which we were going to pilot up the river, when, all of a sudden the wind flied round to the north west with all the fury of a tremendous gale. In fact, it came at us like a clap of thunder, and we were almost blinded with rain at the same time, besides being pitchy dark. Our boat at once became perfectly unmanageable, and we could do nothing but drive back with the boat at the mercy of the sea, which nearly swamped us. We were driven up the river at great speed against the Huntspill sea wall, and as soon as the boat struck we managed to jump ashore. In less than two minutes afterwards, my boat was again dashed against the wall with tremendous violence and knocked into a thousand pieces.' The two men walked back to Burnham, and despite their near-fatal ordeal, joined the crew of the Burnham lifeboat, the *John Godfrey Morris*, which had just been summoned.

During the storm, the Burnham lifeboat had been on standby, but in the pitch black of the storm, no one could establish whether any vessels were in trouble. However, in the first light of Wednesday morning, the fate of several ships could be seen. The steamer *Tender* was capsized off Burnham, two vessels were sunk in the river just below Highbridge Pill, a ketch and another sailing ship could be seen in possible trouble some 5 miles distant beyond Steart Flats, and the steamer *Bulldog* was ashore on Berrow Sands.

Mr G. B. Sully, the Lloyds' agent, and Mr Stoate, the secretary of the Lifeboat Institution at Burnham, considered that more than one lifeboat was needed, but when at six o'clock they sought to telegraph the lifeboat stations at Watchet and Weston-super-Mare, to their surprise the Postmaster advised that under Post Office Regulations contact by wire could not be made before eight o'clock under any circumstance. However, all was not lost, and following the Postmaster's suggestion, the officials of the Great Western Railway at Highbridge provided telegraphic communication with the two towns, and the *C.H. Kingston* was launched from Watchet and the *John Holt* from Weston-super-Mare.

The *John Godrey Morris* was launched from Burnham at about a quarter-past six with George Clapp and William Howe in the twelve-man crew. Although the full fury of the storm had abated, the wind was still blowing hard and the seas heavy as the lifeboat, under sail, tacked up the river to the wrecks of the two coal ketches. Establishing that the crews were safe, the lifeboat returned down-river and made for the vessels seen in trouble out in the bay. However, it was not until about nine o'clock that the Burnham lifeboat finally came alongside the first which was identified as the ketch *Hereford*. Wallowing in the heavy breakers but still anchored, the ketch appeared to be abandoned, and after taking the *John Godfrey Morris* in as close as he dared, Coxswain Alfred Hunt satisfied himself that there was no one on board, and the three-man crew and the ship's boat were missing. The *Hereford*'s sails had been torn away and the deck swept clear, but because of the breaking waves, it was deemed too dangerous to put men aboard and take the ketch into harbour.

The Burnham lifeboat then set out for the second vessel seen in distress, and the mystery of the *Tom* was solved. The sloop, still with the small sail set, had refloated during the night, and been blown into Stolford Bay. With a number of the lifeboatmen as temporary crew, the *Tom* was sailed back to Burnham.

The Weston-super-Mare lifeboat had stood off the *Bulldog* until it was confirmed that her crew were safe, and the Watchet lifeboat stood by their Burnham colleagues at the *Hereford* and *Tom*.

Later on Wednesday, the *Hereford* ran onto the Steart Flats and broke up in the surf. Her boat was found smashed against the Huntspill sea wall, but of Captain Thomas Guy and Amos Rawles and William Daunton, his crew, there was no sign. The engineer of the steamship *Tender* was also missing.

On Friday 4 October, the body of William Daunton was found on Steart Island by George Clapp, the Burnham pilot, who also identified the corpse of the man he had known for over twenty-five years. At the inquest which followed in Highbridge, there was speculation on the fate of the crew of the *Hereford*. They could have been swept off the ketch by the heavy seas and drowned, or lost in the ship's boat. No one could ever know, and a verdict of 'Found Drowned' was returned on the corpse of William Daunton.

A week after the storm, the body of Captain Thomas Guy was found in the River Parrett near Combwich, and the corpse of Amos Rawles recovered off Steart. At both inquests, the speculation of the fate of the two men continued, but once again the result was inconclusive, swept off the *Hereford* or lost in the ship's boat. Verdicts of 'Found Drowned' were returned.

The badly decomposed corpse of the fourth man to be lost in the storm off Burnham, the engineer of the *Tender*, George Harding, was recovered many miles up the River Parrett at Burrow Bridge on 17 October. Identification was by the clothing and stature of the engineer, and the verdict of the inquest was 'Accidentally drowned through the upsetting of the *Tender* steamship for which no one was to blame.'

The *Tender* was salvaged, and after a refit, gave many years service to her owners, Messrs Sully & Co. of Bridgwater, until she was broken up in 1942.

BREAKFAST AT COOMBE VILLA

One of the hidden fears of the employers of servants in the nineteenth century almost came to pass in Mrs Fry's boarding school at Coombe Villa in the village of Monckton Coombe near Bath, when fourteen-years-old Elizabeth Vince put something nasty into her mistress's breakfast arrowroot and found herself standing before Mr Justice Park at the Somerset Spring Assizes in April 1827 charged with administering poison with intent to murder Mrs Tereza Eliza Fry.

In the autumn of 1826, Elizabeth Vince, a pauper, had been placed in service at Coombe Villa with the intention of making her an apprentice by the overseers of the poor of the Parish of Walcot and a few weeks later some sugar of lead was brought to treat the eyes of a gentleman lodger. One afternoon a few weeks later, Elizabeth brought some of the sugar of lead for her mistress saying that it was burnt alum to treat Mrs Fry's baby's ulcerated mouth. Horrified, Mrs Fry snatched the purported medicine from the girl and put it into a packet on which she wrote 'Rank Poison', and locked it away on the top shelf of the cupboard in the breakfast room.

On the morning of 4 December, Mrs Fry sat down to breakfast and Elizabeth brought her daily basin of arrowroot saying that the cook had left it to her mistress to sweeten it. Noticing what seemed to be water floating on the surface of the porridge-like food she asked why the cook had added water but the young servant replied that she had seen it made and only milk had been put in. Mrs Fry took the first spoonful but finding it sweet, enquired why Elizabeth had said that it was unsweetened. She ate another spoonful but found that the arrowroot now tasted acid, a flavour similar to cream of tartar, and the cook was summoned to explain what was going on. Puzzled by the complaint the cook denied adding anything to the arrowroot, indeed she had eaten what was left in the saucepan and it had tasted very good. To prove her point she ate a teaspoonful from the basin but agreed that it had a very unusual flavour. Shortly after both the cook and Mrs Fry were seized with violent stomach cramps and for a while were quite ill. Mrs Fry suspected that all was not well and that someone had tampered with the arrowroot. Going to the breakfast parlour cupboard she found that the packet containing the sugar of lead was missing and so was the small box of oxalic acid, another very nasty poison used in those days as a bleaching and cleaning agent.

To confirm his wife's suspicions, Mr Fry hastened into Bath with the basin containing the remains of the arrowroot which he gave to Mr Day, a surgeon, who confirmed that something had been added and suggested that he take it to Mr Cuff, one of the city's chemists for analysis.

Back at Coombe Villa, Elizabeth Vince was being subjected to strict questioning by a now recovered Mrs Fry, but after vehemently denying adding anything to the arrowroot she accused the cook. Bursting into tears Elizabeth confessed to seeing the cook take something out of a small packet, place it in a cup and then pour some arrowroot on top of it. The cook had then mixed it together, adding that she would tell it again on oath. The cook emphatically denied everything, pointing out that she had eaten some arrowroot and suffered the same as her mistress.

The questioning of Elizabeth Vince continued and finally, she broke down confessing to taking two packets from the cupboard and adding the sugar of lead to the arrowroot; the other packet she had thrown away. She was taken before two local magistrates who sent the girl for trial at the next assizes.

The Frys could not understand why Elizabeth had acted as she did for they believed that she had been treated with kindness, even though a few small articles had gone missing since she joined the household. However, a few days before the events of 4 December, Mrs Fry had mentioned the losses to a friend who had suggested a visit to the 'conjuring man' who would show her the guilty person in a glass.

The trial of Elizabeth Vince opened before Mr Justice Park and Mr Gunning the prosecuting counsel outlined the events leading up to the charge and then told the judge that there was some doubt whether the basin containing the arrowroot was the same as the one delivered to Surgeon Day. The judge ordered the chemist, Mr Cuff, to the witness box to explained what had happened. The chemist stated that he had analysed the contents of the basin given to him by Mr Fry, but had found no sign of sugar of lead or oxalic acid in the mixture. As the basin had passed through so many hands, it was impossible to identify it and its contents as being the same as that given to Mrs Fry.

On hearing this evidence, Mr Justice Park stopped the trial ruling that it would be impossible to arrive at a safe conviction and Elizabeth Vince was acquitted. However, the judge had not finished with Elizabeth and told her that after reading the depositions of the witnesses, he had no doubt that she had committed the crime for which she had been charged and she was a very lucky girl. If it had been proved that the crime was committed and despite her tender age she would have been sentenced to death as an example to 'deter others from such enormous wickedness'.

Young Elizabeth Vince appeared before Mr Justice Park at the Somerset Spring Assizes held in Taunton Castle in April 1827.

DEATH AT ILCHESTER GAOL

Today looking west from Ilchester Bridge it is almost impossible to conceive that on the right bank of the River Yeo there stood for several hundred years the gaunt walls of the County Gaol. It is also almost impossible to imagine the scene on the day when a prisoner (sometimes more than one) was publicly executed by hanging and the large crowd who would pack the left-hand river bank, the bridge and some even sitting on their horses in the river, to gawk at the grizzly spectacle of a man or woman depart this life struggling on the end of a rope.

Ilchester Gaol was closed in 1843 when the County Gaol was opened at Taunton and the gaunt walls and buildings were demolished.

Until 1811 when the 'new drop' was constructed over the entrance block of the gaol, executions by hanging took place in a field known as Gallows Field on the west side of the Ilchester to Yeovil road and to which the unfortunate malefactor would be taken on the back of a cart. In Ilchester on the day of the execution at Gallows Field and later on the 'new drop', there would be something of a carnival atmosphere and the drinking and generally riotous behaviour which accompanied these occasions were commonly called 'hang fairs'.

The unfortunate who would have the dubious 'privilege' of being the first to be hanged on the 'new drop' was sixty-years-old Joseph Bragg who ended his life on 21 April 1813 sentenced to die for setting fire to his brother-in-law's house at East Brent. And strange to relate, the last to pay the ultimate penalty was Daniel Case who was hanged on 1 September 1836 for setting fire to a dwelling house at Templecombe!

The local newspapers at the time would often give quite graphic descriptions of the hangings at the gaol and the last days of the condemned as we can read in the following account from the *Western Flying Post* of 6 May 1822:

'EXECUTIONS-On Wednesday last, *William Darch* for setting fire to a dwelling house, *Benjamin Day*, for a burglary, *Benjamin Glover* and *George Puddy*, for housebreaking, were executed on the drop erected on Ilchester Gaol, pursuant to the sentences passed on them at the late Somerset Assizes. On the previous Sunday, Mr Hardy received a reprieve for *William Abbott*, convicted of highway robbery, who was to have suffered with them. Since their condemnation they had behaved with becoming resignation, and by repentance prepared themselves for their approaching fate, Darch, who was a native of Milverton had, up to the period of the offence of which he was sentenced, borne a good character, and of this crime he declared himself to innocent to the last. Glover was only sixteen, and was a child of a notorious thief in the City of Bath, by whom he had been educated in every species of crime. At the Spring Assizes for 1821 he had been sentenced to death for a burglary, but had been reprieved, and his punishment commuted to a short period of imprisonment. A few days prior to his death he was heard to say, "He cared not for the execution of his sentence, only he feared his d-d heart was not correct." Day and Puddy were both bad characters – The Rev. Mr Valantine, the chaplain of the gaol, was unremitting in his attentions to the unfortunate men, and on the last sabbath they were to pass on earth preached a most impressive discourse from the 8th chapter of Ecclesiastes, v. 13; "But it shall not be well with the wicked neither shall he prolong his days which are a shadow because he feareth not God." About 10 o'clock Mr Melliar, the Under Sheriff having arrived, the criminals were removed from their cells to the chapel where the Sacrament was administered to them; and at half past eleven the awful preparations having been completed they were conducted to the platform, preceded by the clergyman reading the burial service. The absurd custom of retaining the fetters and handcuffs until after the execution, was on this occasion humanely dispensed with, and they were merely pinioned. They all behaved with great firmness and earnestly joined in prayer with the chaplain; after a short time in devotions, the signal was given and they were launched into eternity. The spectators were unusually numerous and consisted (as is usual in such instances) of three females to one man; their behaviour was disgraceful in the extreme, their brutal shouts and mirth even disturbing the administrators of the last Holy Sacrament.'

William Bridle, the governor of Ilchester Gaol 1808-1821.

THE TRAGIC DEATH OF GUNNER SIMS

Gunner William Sims of 141 (The Queen's Own Dorset Yeomanry) Royal Artillery, was home on ten days compassionate leave on 23 May 1945 when tragically he died following a freak accident on the Pen Mill railway bridge.

On 1 June, the *Western Gazette* wrote that the twenty-seven-years-old gunner, living with his wife Gwendoline at 25 Brunswick Street, had gone to meet a friend at Pen Mill Station but was fatally injured by a War Department lorry.

Reporting on the inquest into the cause of the gunner's death, the *Gazette* stated that it was probably due to the lorry hitting a slight depression in the road about 20 yards from the bridge on the Sherborne side. The coroner was informed that:

'The clip of the spring holding the crank rod had come off and the sudden depression had jerked the rod out of place, rendering the steering useless. The lorry crashed into the bridge on which Sims was leaning, dragging him nearly fifty feet into a hedge the other side. He died three hours later.

'Mrs Gwendoline Dora Sims, said her husband had told her he was going to the station to meet a friend to whom he wanted to give a message. Dr Ernst Steiner, house surgeon, Yeovil Hospital, said the cause of death was injuries to the brain and shock caused by a fractured base of the skull.

'Robert John Tutton (fifteen), of 18 Glenville Road who was on the bridge, Brian John Lumbard, 93 Ilchester Road, who was nearby with two other friends, and Mr Gilbert Charles Norman, 7 Vincent Street, gave evidence.

Gunner Sims died in a freak accident on the railway bridge overlooking Pen Mill Station.

'Lance-Corporal Margaret Sadler, A.T.S., who was riding with the lorry driver, described how the driver desperately wrestled with the wheel. But it had no effect and he jammed on his brakes.

'The driver, Ronald William Oliver, a civilian driver attached to the R.A.O.C., Sherborne, said he had no previous trouble with the lorry or its steering. When he was a few yards away from the bridge the wheel went loose and he subsequently found that the crank rod had come out of its groove.

'Sergeant Fermor, Yeovil police, said by giving it a sharp tap upwards the socket of the steering arm came away from the socket of the ball joint, thus rendering it defective. He thought it probable that it became disconnected through a sharp depression in the road. There was no carelessness, he thought, and no negligence.

'The Coroner, Mr C.J.P.C. Jowett, returning a verdict of "Misadventure" thanked the witnesses for the way they had given their evidence. He especially congratulated the two boys who, he said, had been of great service. Supt Hanham, representing the Police, also expressed his appreciation. Lumbard, he said, had greatly assisted the police by taking the number of the lorry.

'The funeral took place at Yeovil Cemetery on Tuesday afternoon. The coffin was covered with the Union Jack and six comrades under a Sergeant-Major acted as bearers. The Rev. Frank Buffard (Baptist Minister) officiated.'

But for an army truck's chance encounter with a sharp depression in the road and the subsequent chain of events, Gunner Sims would have gone home to Gwendoline in Brunswick Street instead of which he now lies in the Commonwealth War Graves Commission's plot at Yeovil Cemetery.

A BATTLE WITH POACHERS

In 1841, the year of the tale which follows, poachers could be divided, generally speaking, between poor countrymen struggling to exist and feed their families on a pauper's wage, and gangs, organised or otherwise, who usually poached game for profit or gain, and who could be ruthless in pursuing their objectives. Whatever the reason, the illegal hunting and trapping of game attracted severe penalties and extreme measures on the part of landowners determined to protect their living property. In addition to the chance of capture by gamekeepers and the authorities, the poacher could suffer maiming in the jaws of a vicious man-trap, or death or severe wounding from the contents of a spring gun fired by a hidden trip-wire. However, despite the penalties and the risks, poaching was not diminished to any great extent, and as many of the participants were known and often highly regarded as local heroes, the authorities could not expect too much co-operation in bringing some poachers to justice.

At the Somerset Spring Assizes held in Taunton in April 1841, the following case of poaching at Pilton came before the Honourable Mr Justice Erskine, and in the dock were four local men indicted for 'entering a close of the Rev. Mr. Wickham in the parish of Pilton, they being armed, with intent to destroy game and having assaulted a constable, to prevent that lawful apprehension'. The four, all of whom pleaded not guilty, were thirty-four-years-old Stephen Millard, John Smith nineteen, James Smith twenty-four, and twenty-years-old Jonathon Hurd.

The three poachers were remanded to Shepton Mallet Gaol to await their trial at the Somerset Spring Assizes in April 1841.

The first witness for the prosecution was the Reverend Mr Wickham's gamekeeper, Emannuel Day who testified that on Monday 9 November (1840) he was in Ham-wood with James Tucker and George Parker as he believed there could be poachers about the area. He lived in a cottage near the wood and the party left at about nine o'clock that evening and after setting up a 'mock pheasant' in a tree about 300 yeards from the path through the wood they took cover.

Early the following morning at about one o'clock whistles were heard nearby and in the moonlight five men were seen approaching the tree and seeing the mock pheasant one of the men raised the gun he was carrying and fired. In the instance of the flash, the gamekeeper saw that one of the other men carried a gun and a third a cudgel. At this moment Emannuel Day described how they had burst out of their hide and he had 'collared two of them, John Smith was one of those I collared, and Millard was the other, I had known John Smith about seven years'. He had then been struck a violent blow to the back of his head but despite being dazed he had held on to John Smith. However, Millard had broken free and began hitting him about the head with the butt end of the gun he was carrying. Despite being badly beaten the gamekeeper managed to defend himself with his stout stick to such extend that Millard broke off his attack and with his other associates who were fighting the gamekeeper's companions 'retreated a short distance'. Millard and Jonathon Hurd suddenly charged the keepers and in the following scrap, John Smith broke free and escaped,

Emannuel Day told the court that Millard and Hurd had suddenly broken off the fight and all five poachers had retreated about a dozen yards from where they shouted threats and one called out to rush the keepers and kill them. The gamekeeper went on to say that 'my party retreated 100 yards, and he saw no more of the poachers. A subsequent search of the site of the fight revealed a broken stock of a gun. Following the fight, he had found that James Tucker was bleeding badly from the wounds he had received and that as a consequence of the blows inflicted to his head the witness had been unwell for a fortnight.

Next into the witness box to give evidence was James Tucker, gamekeeper to Mr Tudway of Wells. He described going into Ham-wood with Emannuel Day and George Parker, waiting near the tree where the mock pheasant had been placed, observing the five poachers, seeing the gun fired into the tree and the Reverend Mr Witcombe's gamekeeper seize James Smith and Stephen Millard. James Tucker went on to describe how he had taken hold of Jonathon Hurd who had 'beaten down the knuckles of my left hand and he had been badly beaten about the head by an unidentified assailant. He had heard the shouts of rush them and kill them and after retreating with Emannuel Day and George Parker he discovered that he was covered in blood. He had been attended by a 'medical man' and still felt the effects of his injuries.

The third prosecution witness was George Parker from Wells who testified that he had accompanied the two gamekeepers on the night in question, recalled seeing Stephen Millard strike Emannuel Day and he had been struck several times by an unidentified attacker.

Thus ended the case for the prosecution and now it was the turn of the defence counsel to address the court. The evidence of the three prosecution witnesses was questioned but could not have satisfied the jury because all four were found guilty as charged.

The *Taunton Courier* of 7 April 1841 reporting on the trial wrote that before passing sentence the judge the Honourable Mr Justice Eskine addressed the four prisoners as follows:

'You have all been found guilty of the same offence, which was accompanied by and with great violence towards those who were authorised by law to apprehend you, and it is highly necessary to put a check on these offences, not for the sake of those protecting game, but the lives of the keepers which are at stake in the lawful enterprise of their duty, and to prevent such persons as you from following any longer in your ill course. As for you Stephen Millard, you committed the offence under very aggravated circumstances, and I have reason to believe that you are a man who has for a length of time been engaged in such transactions. The sentence of this Court is that you be transported for seven years; and the sentence of the Court on you John Smith, James Smith and Jonathon Hurd is, that you be imprisoned and kept to hard labour for eighteen calendar months.'

And who was the fifth man involved in the poaching expedition? If he was known, he was never arrested and brought to trial, and it seems that his name was never revealed by his four companions in crime. He was, therefore, a very lucky man.

ALL GUNS ARE DANGEROUS

Guns of all shapes and sizes, from the small pocket pistol to the largest artillery piece if not handled properly and with respect can be extremely dangerous as the following tragic fatal events will testify.

The Golden Jubilee of King George III would be celebrated with a bang by the local Volunteers at Galhampton, near Castle Cary, on 25 October 1809. The Volunteers commanded by Colonel Woodforde had placed a battery of cannon near Galhampton House to fire salutes to the monarch on entering the fiftieth year of his reign. The Volunteers were not to be denied the Jubilee rejoicings and were attending a public dinner in Castle Cary together with the other festivities in the town. Captain John Burge had been given responsibility for the care of the battery and had left Thomas Millard, a member of his Company, together with another Volunteer, in charge of the guns.

No officer or NCO was left to supervise the two Volunteers, and it would seem that they became bored and Thomas Millard decided to light the touch-hole of one of the cannon as a jolly jape. However, the gun did not fire, and so Millard took a ramrod and standing in front of the muzzle, thrust it down the barrel whilst the touch-hole was still smouldering. The result was a foregone conclusion because the cannon immediately discharged and the unfortunate but foolish Thomas Millard, busily pushing the ramrod down the barrel', was blown to pieces. The remains of poor Volunteer Millard, some of which had been propelled for some distance, were collected up, and what was left of the twenty-four-years-old deceased were buried in the parish churchyard on 29 October 1809.

Fifty-seven years later on Thursday 2 August 1866, there would be another celebration but this time to mark the occasion in Langport of the marriage of Margaret, the second daughter of the town's prominent banker and shipowner, Edward Bagehot, to George Porch, a Glastonbury banker.

Some Langport boatmen and their friends had been permitted to celebrate the wedding by firing salutes from an old muzzle-loading cannon owned by Messrs. Bagehot & Co. The cannon was placed in the company's coal yard on the bank of the River Parrett next to Langport Bridge and manned by boatman George Davidge, Walter Webb a veteran Royal Marine and now armoury sergeant of the 21st Somerset Rifle Volunteers, Sergeant Grimes, the Rifle Volunteers' drill instructor, and another former Royal Marine, boatman Robert Beck.

The veteran Royal Marine Walter Webb had charge of the cannon and Sergeant Grimes was responsible for preparing the powder charges and placing them at the mouth of the barrel for Webb and Davidge to ram home. However, there was no proper rammer to scour and sponge out the barrel to prevent a spark or fire remaining following each discharge and the men had improvised with a length of wood with a piece of sacking tied at the end to act as the sponge.

For the first salute, Sergeant Grimes filled three tins with gun powder and

The tragic events of 2 August 1866 were enacted on the left bank of the River Parrett looking towards Langport's Bow Bridge.

placed them in the barrel followed by some paper and old clothes to form the wadding and the charge was rammed home by Webb and Davidge. The vent of the cannon was primed by the veteran Royal Marine Robert Beck, the slow match applied to vent, and to the delight of the townsfolk crowding the coal yard and the river bridge, the gun went off with a flash, an almighty bang and a cloud of smoke billowed across the Parrett.

By one o'clock in the afternoon, three salutes had been fired but as Walter Webb and George Davidge rammed home the charges for the fourth, the cannon went off! Both of Webb's arms were blown away close to the elbows and he was hurled unconscious into the river, followed by Davidge who lost an arm and a hand besides receiving severe gashes to his throat and kneck. Sergeant Grimes' face was badly scorched and Beck lost part of the thumb he had placed over the vent to seal it during the loading. Several spectators standing near the front of the cannon to watch the charge being rammed down the barrel were slightly injured from the unexpected muzzle blast.

Despite his appalling injuries, George Davidge managed to haul himself out of the river and lay bleeding on the bank. Ignoring his burns, Sergeant Grimes plunged into the river and dragged the unconscious Walter Webb up the bank. The terribly injured men were carried from the scene, George Davidge to his home, but because of his condition, Walter Webb was taken the short distance to the Dolphin Inn where he died some five hours later despite the efforts of the town's medical men to save him.

The inquest into the death of the veteran Royal Marine was held by the bride's father Edward Bagehot who happened also to be the coroner, in the Langport town hall during the afternoon of the following day. The first witness with his face heavily bandaged, was Sergeant Grimes who described the events leading up to the cannon's fatal discharge. He stated that both Webb and Davidge appeared to know how to manage the gun and the vent was properly stopped by the veteran Royal Marine, Robert Beck. The sergeant thought that some burning rag had been left in the barrel following the previous discharge and this had caused the gun to go off.

Robert Beck followed the sergeant and stated that he had reminded Walter Webb to wet sponge the barrel after the third discharge but this advice had been ignored and the powder charge rammed home. If the barrel had been sponged correctly the accident would not have occurred and as a former Royal Marine, Walter Webb ought to have known how to manage the cannon.

James Holley, a local innkeeper, was called and stated that he had supplied some drink to the men firing the cannon and stayed to watch the proceedings. He had been standing near the gun and had been knocked over by the blast of the fatal discharge. He concluded by saying that the firing party were perfectly sober.

Following this testimony the jury returned a verdict of accidental death and suggested that the cannon should never be used again; they gave their fees to Walter Webb's widow.

The veteran Royal Marine was buried in Huish Episcopi churchyard on Saturday, August and a firing party from the 21st Somerset Rifle Volunteers fired three volleys over the grave. As Walter Webb was being taken to his final resting place, George Davidge succumbed from his terrible injuries.

The size of the firearm is of no account when it comes to not treating it with respect or caution as the following tragedy will reveal.

In the summer of 1940, following the evacuation of the British Expeditionary Force from Dunkirk, there were thousands of armed troops in the country, and even if many of them were experienced in the use of firearms, tragedies were inevitable.

On Tuesday 9 July 1940 an inquest opened at the Yeovil Law Courts, into the death of twenty-one-years-old Driver John Harper of the Royal Army Service Corps who had died at Houndstone Camp from a gunshot wound in his chest.

Witness, Driver Davidson, told the inquest that he had asked his pal, John Harper if he knew how to load a rifle after it had been fully cocked. Replying in the negative, Davidson told him it was easy and was demonstrating the technique when the rifle went off and John Harper fell dead.

The coroner asked Driver Davidson who had taught him this 'silly trick' with the rifle and the witness replied that he had learnt it during his recent service in France.

Summing up, the coroner said that this was a case of 'familiarity breeding contempt' There was no doubt that the tragedy was an accident but it had been caused by orders being disobeyed. He knew that in the last war men used these kinds of tricks, but it was wrong to do so. A verdict of Accidental Death was recorded.

THOMAS PEARCE IS SHOT

Early in the evening of 3 July 1823, Thomas Pearce, one of Lord Glastonbury's gamekeepers, was riding his horse down a lane near land at Compton Dundon rented by the Voke family. Suddenly there was a gunshot and dismounting the gamekeeper walked across several fields towards the sound of the shot and he saw young Samuel Voke reloading his gun. Although the Vokes rented the land from the Glastonbury Estate, the shooting rights were not included and as Thomas Pearce had long suspected Samuel of hunting game on the land he had now caught him red-handed.

The keeper told the young man that he was poaching and as this was a serious offence he would have to report him. Samuel begged to be pardoned, but Thomas Pearce replied that it was no longer within his power to do so. However, Mr Ryall, the estate steward might be prepared to let him off the charge and Samuel Voke agreed to go with the keeper to the steward's house.

The two men walked together across the fields but just before they reached the lane, Thomas Pearce went on ahead to fetch his horse. Suddenly there was a bang from behind, and the keeper felt a blow like the kick from a horse, Samuel Voke had fired his loaded gun into the man's back and then made off.

Thomas Pearce was a very lucky man because his thick loose clothes absorbed most of the shot. However, the force of the shot had severely bruised his back and thinking it to be broken the keeper did not pursue his attacker and after painfully and with much difficulty mounting his horse, began to make his slow way home. The injured man had not gone more than half a mile when without warning his horse shied as a figure emerged from behind a large ash tree growing less than four yards away on the right-hand side of the lane. Thomas Pearce had time to recognise Samuel

Following the shooting of Thomas Pearse, Samuel Voke fled from Compton Dundon.

Voke and to look down the barrel of his gun before it was fired blasting away the keeper's right eye, seven teeth and parts of his cheek and neck. Miraculously the sixty-six-years-old man was not fatally wounded but managed to retain his seat and ride the mile and a half to the steward's house. Here Mr Ryall helped the grievously wounded keeper down from his horse and after applying poultices to the wounds, sent for a surgeon. For several days Thomas Pearce's life hung in the balance, but he had a strong constitution and made a slow recovery.

Meanwhile, the search was on for Samuel Voke who had fled from his home at Compton Dundon, but within a few days, he was arrested in Hallatrow, near Midsomer Norton.

One month later Samuel Voke appeared at the Somerset Summer Assizes in Bridgwater charged with the hanging offence of maliciously and wilfully shooting at Thomas Pearce with intent to murder him. The trial was short, the prisoner found guilty and sentenced to death.

During the time Samuel Voke spent awaiting his fate at Ilchester Gaol he was said to have been truly repentant and on the eve of his execution, Thomas Pearce visited the condemned man and they were reconciled.

At eleven o'clock on the morning of 26 November 1823, Samuel Voke climbed the steps to the platform of the gallows and after praying with the prison chaplain for some fifteen minutes, the rope was fastened around his neck, the white cap was drawn down over his face and the trap fell away.

Samuel Voke was described as being a remarkably fine young man of twenty-one-years and the son of respectable parents who occupied a small farm at Compton Dundon.

We will never know what Samuel was hunting but was it worth dying for?

A TRAGEDY IN THE RIVER YEO

During the evening of Thursday 17 October 1844, James Harris, bailiff to Mr George Harbin of Newton House, fell in the River Yeo near the weir below Wyndham Hill, and John Cridland tried to save him; tragically both drowned.

The *Western Flying Post* reported that Mr Caines, the Coroner, held the Inquest on the bodies of the two men in the Pen Mill Hotel on the following Saturday, and the first witness to give evidence was Mr George Harbin who testified that:

'On Thursday last men to the number of twenty were employed in emptying the water of the weir pool of the River Yeo near Pen Mill and to carry out repairs to the weir; there were several volunteers, and work was proceeding with great energy. They began about ten and at about half past five, being present myself, I desired the men to cease from work, and partake of some refreshment that had been provided for them in a tent near where they had been working. All the men at the time appeared to be sober – they had had sufficient liquor, but did not appear to be in a state of intoxication. Harris, as my bailiff, had been looking on as a spectator, and he had nothing to do with the work. Between three and four I desired him to go the Brewery and purchase some beer for the men, and it seems that at the Brewery he had two small glasses of beer given to him. At half past five I desired the men to desist, upon which they had all said they had better finish their job that night, I was however anxious they should cease, as it was getting late, and the men, in obedience to my directions got out of the water and went to the tent. I saw Cridland at the time, and he observed to me that I had better have the fish taken out of the pool that night, showing by this remark that he was perfectly aware of what he was doing. I took the precaution of asking George Bradley to preserve order amongst the men during the absence of my servant James Meech, but wrangling and dispute took place after they had had their first cup of liquor, and there was rather an inclination to fight. My servant went to the tent and said no more liquor would be drawn that night if they kept quarrelling upon which they agreed to shake hands and make it up. About quarter past seven, when I was at my dinner table, my servant rushed into the room calling out "Dear Sir something dreadful has happened, for God's sake come, two men are drowned. The boat, the boat!" I ran as quick as I could, got into the boat and took my servant with me, and rowed from Newton to the spot in about ten minutes. Some men were trying to get up the bodies with a crook when we got to the spot; my servant, took the crook, and in about five minutes brought up the body of George Cridland. I directed them to take the body immediately to Pen-mill, the nearest place, to wrap it in blankets, and get immediate medical assistance. This was done, and we continued our search; from five to ten minutes elapsed and then my servant, James Meech, succeeded in bringing to the surface the body of poor Harris. With the aid of those present we brought the body down to the mill where I ascertained that they had placed the other body in the hay-loft; I had it brought down immediately, and both bodies taken into the kitchen of the mill, whilst a fire was lit in the bake-house. Before the surgeon came every effort was made to restore animation, but our endeavours were useless; I should think they had been more than half an hour in the water. Harris was not addicted to liquor and the whole time he was in my employ for six years I never saw him intoxicated.'

The next to give evidence was George Bradley, a dairyman, who told the Inquest that he had been placed in charge of the work in the absence of James Meech, Mr Harbin's servant. The men had drunk about two cups of beer each, but he did not think they were drunk. James Harris, the bailiff, had drunk a little quantity of beer but was perfectly in control of his senses. The witness stated that he had seen the bailiff some ten minutes before he heard a splash from the river above the weir.

Carpenter, Hugh Slade, testified that at about seven he had been walking along the footpath on the opposite bank of the river and had heard shouting and arguing coming from the tent. He had stopped to listen, and in the moonlight he saw James Harris come out of the tent and walk straight into the river. Seeing the bailiff struggling in the water, Hugh Slade stated that he had shouted for help and men had come running from the tent. The carpenter described how John Cridland had run to the river and 'without taking off even his hat, jumped in. He took the other man by the back, and pulled him back towards the bank; neither of them spoke and they both went to the bottom.'

Recalled by the coroner, Mr Harbin explained that James Harris had, 'An affliction of the eyes for which he was surgically attended, and no doubt he had mistook his path and slipped into the river.' Mr Harbin felt it was a pity the men had apparently forgotten that there were ropes and a pole near at hand, but had run instead to his house for the boat.

The coroner stated that he considered there was no need to call any further witnesses because it was quite evident how the two men had died, and as there was no evidence of intoxication. The inquest Jury returned a verdict of accidental death in the case of James Harris, and John Cridland had perished in the attempt to rescue him.

The River Yeo and the Newton House boathouse and boat.

Subscriptions were raised to help the families of the two men – James Harris left a wife and five grown-up children and the younger man, John Cridland left a widow and two small children in Bradford Abbas

DEATH AT DEADMAN'S POST

Twelve-years-old John had an awful life, he was severely undernourished, weak, sickly and suffered regular beatings from his brutal father, James Lane, a small farmer. It would all come to a terrible conclusion in the spring of 1830 on the Blackdown Hills in his home at the sinisterly named Deadman's Post.

It was in the early evening of 23 April in the year 1830, that John Ball was returning over Staple Hill to his home at Buckland St Mary when he saw James Lane standing by the hedge of his potato field.

'Come over,' the farmer called. 'I've a dead fellow here!'

'Who is it?' enquired the puzzled John Ball as he clambered over the hedge.

'T'is our Jack,' replied Farmer Lane pointing to the small figure of a boy huddled face down on the wet earth.

Kneeling by the small form, John turned it over and saw it was the farmer's young son John and was relieved to find that he was breathing.

'Come on lad stand up,' he whispered.

'I can't,' was the reply. 'I've tried and I can't'.

John Ball raised the lad and sat him back against the hedge bank. At this, the farmer took over and shouted 'If you don't get over thik hedge I'll take a good stick to 'ee!'

When the boy failed to move, Lane grabbed his collar, hauled him up on to the top of the hedge bank, and threw his son down some 6 feet into the water-filled ditch below.

Horrified, John Ball scrambled after the child and gently pulling him out of the ditch, laid him down on the grass by the side of the road. When Lane joined them, he pulled the semi-conscious lad to his feet and punched him hard on his forehead.

By now three other local men, James Cross, James Quick and George Bryant had arrived and witnessed the beating. James Lane brought his horse from the potato field and threw young John across its back but after travelling a few yards, the boy lost what small grip he had on the reins and began to slide off. Dragging his son off he tossed him over his shoulder and carried the boy to their home at Deadman's Post.

At seven o'clock the next morning, 24 April, John Lane's short and miserable life came to an end, and two days later an inquest was held into his death at the Castle Inn on Neroche Hill. On hearing the evidence of the witnesses to the assault on the boy and the medical testimony of two Chard surgeons, the jury returned a verdict of wilful murder against James Lane, he was arrested and committed to Ilchester Gaol to await trial.

Pleading not guilty, James Lane went on trial four months later on 20 August at the Somerset Summer Assizes in Wells, charged with the 'wilful murder of John Lane by inflicting blows, throwing him to the ground with violence and not providing him with sufficient food'. The trial would reveal a story of beatings, starvation and the awful treatment of the farmer's son over many years; death may well have come as a friend.

The principal prosecution witness was John Ball who described the brutal events on Staple Hill and as he had accompanied James Lane and his son back to Deadman's Post, told of the events which followed.

On entering the farmhouse, Lane had dropped the boy onto the floor shouting that he was a sulky beggar and that he would never pick him up again. Hearing the commotion, the boy's mother Ann, appeared and picking him up placed the lad near the fire to warm and dry his soaking wet clothes. Now the true horror began, Lane grabbed his son and placed his head within some three inches of the flames shouting 'I'll see whether he'll move now or not!' The boy screamed in fear and pain but was too weak to move his head away from the scorching heat. John Ball described how he had pulled the lad away from the fire and back to where his mother had laid him. Lane, however, had not finished with his son but dragged him to the opposite end of the room away from any warmth muttering that the boy should not lie there comforting himself. The witness closed his evidence by saying that he had told Lane in no uncertain terms that he should not treat John in this way and should put him in a warm bed as he feared the boy might die. In reply, Lane exclaimed that this would be good riddance and he wished the boy dead before morning. A wish which as events turned out had come horribly true.

In a ship similar to the Success, *James Lane was transported to Australia in 1831.*

John Ball was followed into the witness box by the three men who had seen the beating on Staple Hill and a number of people who testified to the prisoner's cruelty to his son over the years.

Because the weight of evidence against James Lane appeared so great and fearing a guilty verdict and the possibility of meeting the hangman at Ilchester Gaol, on the advice of his lawyer, Lane pleaded guilty to manslaughter. The murder charge was dropped, and although James Lane escaped the gallows, he was transported to Australia for life.

The Ilchester Gaol records give us a brief glimpse of James Lane. He was thirty-eight-years of age standing five-feet-six and a half-inches tall of stout frame, had an oval face with a cut on the chin, sandy hair and could read but not write.

He was sent in chains to the Portsmouth prison hulk *Captivity*, and on 22 November 1831, James Lane left Plymouth bound for Australia, one of 225 prisoners on the convict ship *Isabella*, arriving on 25 March 1832 at Port Jackson, which is now part of Sydney Harbour.

A FRIEND AND A FOE

The church of the Holy Cross, Weston Bampfylde, stands on a low hill south of Sparkford and would seem at first glance to be an unlikely candidate for the echoes within its walls of surprising events, political intrigue, government agents, double-dealing and Robinson Crusoe.

On the south wall of the nave, there is a memorial to Grace, the daughter of Matthew and Ann Lydford of Weston Bampfylde, wife of Nathaniel Mist, and who died in 1726, aged thirty-six years at Carter Lane, London. On the memorial her grieving husband penned the following epitaph to his beloved Somerset wife: 'In prisons and dungeons her resolution and fidelity were his comfort and support whilst her mildness and other conjugal vertues sweetn'd his better fortunes.' What did Nathaniel Mist mean when he penned these words for the monument he erected to 'preserve the memory of her who made his life happy.'?

Little is known of the early life of Nathaniel Mist except that he was probably a Wiltshire man by birth and served as an ordinary seaman in the Royal Navy on the Spanish Seas. He first comes to notice when he set up as a printer in Carter Lane in the City of London in 1715, the year following the succession of the Hanoverian George I to the throne of England, and in 1716, Mist founded *The Weekly Journal* supporting the Jacobite cause of the deposed Stuarts. The Jacobites had made a serious attempt in 1715 to place James III, the son of the ill-starred James II and known as the Old Pretender, on the English throne, but the uprising was swiftly suppressed. However, there was continual plotting against George I, and the Jacobites' readiness to advance their cause whenever they could, including the use of anti-government propaganda and journals, was a constant source of anxiety to the government. The Jacobite cause was finally destroyed in 1746, when the Old Pretender's son Bonnie Prince Charlie and his army, were defeated at the Battle of Culloden.

It was into this atmosphere of plot and counterplot, that Nathaniel Mist, the ex-seaman, introduced his Jacobite newssheet, and which was soon selling some 10,000 copies every week to a large proportion of the reading public of the time. Another figure now appears on the scene and becomes the Editor of *Mist's Weekly Journal*; it is the enigmatic Daniel Defoe. As plain Daniel Foe, he was the son of a London butcher and claimed to have ridden with the Duke of Monmouth in the Rebellion of 1685. He trained to be a Dissenting Minister, was a businessman, a bankrupt, a pamphleteer and journalist, the author of *Robinson Crusoe* and *Moll Flanders*, before dying in hiding from his creditors in 1731. Defoe was also a government secret agent serving both Tory and Whig governments at various times! For at least ten years before becoming editor of *Mist's Weekly Journal* in 1716, he had been working as an undercover government agent and it is believed he spent some time in Scotland operating against the Jacobites in 1706 and 1707.

Defoe's mission in joining Nathaniel Mist was to gradually neutralize the *Journal* by softening its Jacobitism and render it harmless without raising the publisher's suspicions. He wrote the anti-government editorials and on one occasion a raid and search of Nathaniel Mist's home produced the originals of the seditious articles in Defoe's handwriting. Later, Defoe would boast that he had so softened the *Journal's* tone that it was becoming useful to the government. Needless to say, even with Defoe writing the articles, Mist could not escape attention, and he was arrested and thrown into gaol or put in the pillory on several occasions for libels against the government. Each time, however, Defoe would intercede for his employer and either obtain his release or the reduction in the severity of the sentence. How could Nathaniel Mist suspect that his loyal editor could be anything but a friend and supporter of the cause?

Although by 1724, Mist had been in and out of gaol several times, he continued to be a thorn in the side of the government, but it was during his last imprisonment that somehow he finally discovered Defoe's duplicity. On his release, an extremely angry Nathaniel Mist went looking for his editor with murder in mind and on finding Defoe, drew his sword and laid into him. In the fight which followed Mist was wounded, and Defoe called a surgeon to dress his opponent's wounds, but whether this was done through pangs of conscience for his one-time colleague, or from the basic fear that if Mist died, he would be in serious trouble, both history and Daniel Defoe are silent. In 1728, some two years after the death of his wife, Mist's position had become very dangerous and now lacking Defoe's protection, he fled to France where he died nine years later from asthma.

The church of the Holy Cross, Weston Bampfylde.

A LONG FORGOTTEN GHOST STORY

This article appeared in the *Chard, Ilminster and Axminster News* in the publication of Saturday 11 February 1890:

'The following interesting account is to be found amongst the "Recollections" (in manuscript) of the late Richard Walter, Esq., formerly of Combe St Nicholas, who died in 1888, at the great age of ninety-nine years. Through the courtesy of Dr W.W. Walter, of Stoke-sub-Hamdon, what is entitled "Woodhouse Mysteries," is now for the first time published:

"In the parish of Knowle [Knowle St Giles] and not far from the North East boundary of Chard Common, was a farmhouse tenanted by a Mr Vincent, which was on the property of Earl Poulett, and called 'Wood House.' From its old style of architecture, it appeared to have been some kind of religious establishment, in in a part of the building was a spacious room open to the roof, which had been apparently a kitchen or refectory. In this was a wide fire-place spanned over with an arched stone chimney-piece. In the wall, on one side, supporting this, was an oven, which seems to prove that it was used as a kitchen.

"In the year 1806, on a dry Easter Sunday, a fire unaccountably broke out in the thatched roof of this building which soon extended to other parts of the dwelling house, and all were reduced to ashes. I happened to be present and assisted at the fire; and feeling much interested in the distress of the family, I went a few days after to the ruins and found labourers clearing away the rubbish.

"Mrs Vincent the farmer's wife, being present, pointed out a particular large paving stone in one of the rooms, and wished to have it taken up, stating the reason for so doing was that she had frequently seen a supernatural figure moving towards the spot, and then disappearing. She excited the ridicule of those present, but as she was serious on the subject and anxious to see what was underneath the stone, it was taken up and there were the decaying bone of a human skeleton, apparently from their size those of a female.

"This discovery encouraged Mrs Vincent to be more communicative, and she declared, in the most serious manner, that both she and others had frequently seen a figure, clad in white come to the bedside and look at those lying there.

"This was to me a source of mirth and ridicule, when she called her daughter, a girl of about eleven years of age, and asked her to tell the gentleman what she had seen in her bedroom. 'What,' says the girl, 'do you mean the white lady? Oh! I have seen her many and many a time come to my bedside. I used to be frightened, but lately did not much care about it.' Her mother seemed much displeased with our laughter, and went on to say, 'she was sure there was something mysterious that had happened there. She then referred to the old kitchen, and stated that she suspected some cavity existed near the oven, which, when heated, would never get red hot like the other parts, and she wished it to be examined. This was done, and in the pier, or wall supporting the chimney-piece adjoining the oven, was a stone

The teller of this strange tale lived in Combe St Nicholas and reached the 'great age of ninety-nine years'.

rather loosened by the heat of the late fire. It was, as far as I can remember, about 20 inches high, and 10 or 12 inches wide, and about four feet from the ground. This stone was removed, and in a recess behind it, was found, what startled us all. There was one lady's slipper, which was embroidered with silver thread, &c., a number of beads, also some bone or ivory rings, with other small articles that I do not recollect; but what surprised us most, was the bones of an infant, which appeared to have been crammed in (not laid out) the cloth in which it may have been wrapped being too much decayed to be described.

"The skeleton appeared to have been that of a very young child. The thigh bone, which (with some others) I took home, was about 6 or 8 inches in length. I thought to have kept these relics, but on the very next day, a messenger came from Lady Poulett with an angry message, requesting me to give them up, which of course I did, with an apology for having taken them away.

"The above is a plain statement of facts, which I do not pretend to account for. As to the buried skeleton, probably as it had been a religious establishment (perhaps a convent) there might be many more bodies buried there, but the bones of a child seem to reveal a dark deed of iniquity, on which I do not wish to dwell, but it may be left to the reader to comment on, and account for, far more charitably than I can.'"

FIRE!

Bower Hinton

Mr Cook's timely passing of Mr Silas Bartlett's house in Bower Hinton, at about half-past seven, on Tuesday evening 11 February 1873, prevented the total destruction of the property when he observed flames shooting up from the rear. He immediately raised the alarm, and within half an hour the Martock fire engine was on the scene. The South Petherton fire brigade and their powerful engine had been called, and on their arrival were soon rendering, in the words of the *Western Gazette*, 'valuable assistance, their abundance length of hose enabling them to use with the greatest effect a large but somewhat distant supply of water. While the Martock engine depended on the efforts of bystanders for the supply on water, the Petherton engine pumped its supply direct from the pond'. The firemen made a fire break by stripping off a portion of the unburned thatched roof, and thus saved about of third of what remained. It appeared that the fire had broken out in a wash-house at the back of the cottage and then spread to the roof. In reporting the blaze the *Gazette* commented that 'It is generally considered that the parish of Martock ought to be provided with a more efficient machine.'

Chard

From the *Bath Chronicle* of 29 March 1827: 'On Sunday morning [18 March 1827] at about 1 o'clock an alarming fire occured in Chard in consequence of the chimney at the Angel Inn having caught fire before Mr Soper the landlord had retired for rest. The flames raged in such a fury that at one time if the wind had not fortunately shifted, a great part of the town would have been in danger of destruction. We regret to add that the Inn and two large dwellinghouses adjoining were burnt to the ground and, what makes it still more distressing, the inmates of the house were obliged to escape almost in a state of nudity.

'A young man named Denning had scarcely time to run down stairs before his house and shop of ironmongers were levelled to the ground, they were not insured. In the adjoining premises, a young woman in a dying state was obliged to be carried to a neighbour's house.

'We are concerned to learn that Mr Soper had no time to save his money, much less his furniture; upwards of £100 in bank notes fell a prey to the flames but we are happy to state that his premises were insured.

'The George Inn was saved by cutting off the communication. The wind being at the time very high, many houses on the other side of the street were obliged to be unroofed having several times taken fire.'

Merriott

The combination of a gun, rats and thatch can result in consequences of a very inflamatory nature. For example, Friday 12 April 1811 would not be forgotten in

Merriott for many years to come, because on that windy spring afternoon, 23 cottages and a large number of outhouses were entirely consumed by a ferocious fire. It was said that the fire began in Mr Murley's malthouse by a man shooting rats in the thatched building, and the flame from the discharge of the gun set the thatch on fire. Whatever the cause, the blaze fanned by a strong wind, rapidly spread and despite the frantic attempts to stop its progress, all 23 cottages were burnt out and 23 families rendered homeless. Four dwellings were completely destroyed leaving only parts of walls standing and there were reports that the buildings were uninsured.

Wrington

In this instance, the combination was a gun, some small birds and the thatch on a barley mow in which the consequences turned out to be the same but not quite on the same scale.. The *Taunton Courier* of Wednesday 10 August 1825 reported that on Monday se'nnight, [31 July] a fire was occasioned at Wrington, by a lad firing at some small birds, which were perched on a barley mow, and the charge lodging in the thatch, it soon ignited and communicated to the farmhouse, which was destroyed, with other property of value, before the flames could be subdued.

Yeovil

For over sixty years, Messrs Aplin and Barrett made cheese and dairy products at their factory in Newton Road and which was also the head office of the firm's several subsidiaries. Aplin and Barrett's most famous product, St Ivel Lactic Cheese, was introduced in 1901 and sold worldwide. The firm was subsequently taken over by the Unigate organisation and in due course, the Newton Road operations were closed down, and the site is now occupied by various business units and residential flats.

At about five o'clock on Sunday afternoon, 11 August 1912, fire broke out in the factory, and by the time the Yeovil Volunteer Fire Brigade arrived on the scene, the blaze was spreading rapidly through the premises. The fire brigade was soon joined and assisted by several directors of the company and many staff turned up to lend a hand and battle to keep the fire contained in the offices and the creamery. Close by the blazing building and next to Wyndham Fields, was a range of buildings containing new and valuable machinery and a large stock of very inflammable material. Behind were the boiler house and the powerhouse containing the large dynamos and engines which provided light and power to the factory and offices. On the other side of the blaze were more offices and stores as well as the *Western Gazette's* offices and printing works. The *Gazette's* Managing Director, Mr J. Trevor-Davies, arrived on the scene and as a former Captain of the Sherborne Fire Brigade, telephoned for assistance from the Sherborne men. A Mr L. Forse immediately motored off to Sherborne and returned with several firemen and equipment to help their Yeovil colleagues. Mr Trevor-Davies also assisted by

Part of the badly fire damaged cheese and dairy products factory on Newton Road.

taking hoses into the rear of the *Gazette's* offices and directing streams of water onto the buildings threatened by the blaze. Luckily there was little wind to fan the flames onto adjoining buildings, and when the roofs fell in, the firemen began to get the upper hand. By seven o'clock all danger of the blaze spreading was passed, but the fire would take several more hours to put out.

News of the fire spread quickly through Yeovil and within a short time a large crowd had collected in Newton Road and Wyndham Fields. However, the company's staff turned out, and despite the extensive damage, Monday saw cheese production up and running, and the office staff accommodated in temporary quarters.,The estimated cost of the blaze was put at £20,000 and it was believed to have been caused by an electric cable becoming overheated.

Two full-time members of the London Fire Brigade had been in Yeovil on that Sunday and helped the local men. One of the firemen, Mr J. W. Rickman, subsequently wrote from the Central Fire Station, Tottenham, to the Editor of the *Western Gazette*:

'Whilst on a visit to Yeovil on Sunday, the 11 instant, I was afforded an opportunity of witnessing the efforts of the local Volunteer Fire Brigade in their endeavour to extinguish the conflagration at Messrs Aplin & Barrett's Works. I must say at once that I was very much impressed with the splendid manner in which the Brigade worked, and I cannot refrain from saying that the way in which they tackled the job reflected a great credit upon them and would have been an object lesson even for professional firemen. The police, as usual, were well to the fore and for the valuable assistance and strenuous labour they rendered, deserve justifiable praise. I may perhaps be excused for passing my observation, but 12 years service as a fireman and 10 years with the present Brigade, enable me to form my judgment from a somewhat larger outlook, and I may say in passing, that as I worked beside the men on this occasion in a voluntary capacity I had an excellent opportunity of forming an opinion. I was due back to duty the same evening, or I should dearly liked to have remained until the close of the job.' Praise indeed.

LOST AT SEA

The two following stories may have happened many miles distant from the borders of Somerset but both involved people and families from the Land of Summer.

The loss of HMS *Serpent*.

On the inside of the north wall of St Mary's church, Chilthorne Domer, there is a brass memorial to Frank Holsgrove, which reads – 'One of the Officers of HMS SERPENT wrecked off the north coast of Spain on November 10th 1890 – Placed by his grieving widow.'

The grieving widow was Sarah, the daughter of Chilthorne Domer dairyman Mr George Hann, and wife of thirty-five-years-old Frank Holsgrove, a native of Exeter, the Head Gunner on the Archer-class Torpedo Cruiser HMS *Serpent*.

The cruiser had been launched just two years before in 1888, carried a complement of 176 officers and ratings, was armed with six 6-inch guns, eight 3-pounder quick firers, two machine guns and three 14-inch torpedo tubes; she was also the first vessel in the Royal Navy to be galvanised to protect her metal plates from salt water corrosion.

On Saturday 8 November 1890, *Serpent,* sailed from Devonport bound for the West African Station at Sierra Leone to relieve HMS *Acorn*, and two nights later was off Punta del Buey, on the north west coast of Spain. The night was pitch black, there was a heavy sea running with a strong on-shore current, and driving rain in the gale-force wind. The *Serpent* was travelling at half speed through the stormy night when she drove onto the Punta Buey reef at about half-past ten, the cruiser was some 10 miles off course, probably due to a faulty compass, and broke up in the enormous waves crashing onto the rocks. Of the complement of 176 officers and ratings, only three sailors survived to struggle onto the gale lashed shore.

During the days which followed, the bodies of the men of the *Serpent* were washed ashore, and now lie buried in a small cemetery enclosure near the village of Camarinas overlooking the sea and the reef on which the cruiser foundered on 10 November 1890; a tragedy echoed on the brass memorial on the north wall of St Mary's church, in the Somerset village of Chilthorne Domer and in the columns of both local newspapers the *Western Gazette* and *Western Chronicle* of 14 and 21 November 1890.

Also lost in the wreck of the *Serpent* was Private James Napper of the Royal Marine Light Infantry who hailed from the village of Stoford, near Yeovil.

The wreck of the *Mohegan*

Eight years later, the Atlantic Transport Company's new fast ocean liner *Mohegan* left London bound for New York on her second transatlantic crossing during the afternoon of Thursday 13 October 1898. The *Mohegan* was a modern and extremely luxurious 'all first class' ship of some 3750 tons, 475 feet in length, and capable of a top speed of 13 knots from her triple expansion steam engines. On 13 October she was carrying 53 first class passengers and 97 crew under the command of Captain Griffiths, the Commodore of the Atlantic Transport line.

The voyage down the English Channel was in the teeth of a strong south-westerly wind and steep seas, but these conditions could be well handled by the liner. Just before 7 o'clock on the Friday evening, the *Mohegan* was approaching the Lizard, it was dark but clear, and the passengers were assembling in the saloon for dinner. Without warning the liner, now travelling at full speed, crashed onto the treacherous Manacles Reef; the *Mohegan* was some 10 to 15 miles off course! The huge gash torn below the waterline was so devastating that the watertight compartments were useless. The engine room was immediately flooded and the electric lights failed, plunging the liner into darkness.

The passengers rushed on deck to find it being swept by breakers as the stricken *Mohegan* rocked to and fro on the reef and began to list. Captain Griffiths managed to fire several distress flares but only two of the ship's life-boats could be launched before the liner lurched and sank, throwing the crew and those passengers who had not escaped in the boats, into the boiling surf. All that remained of the *Mohegan* was the top of her funnel and the tops of her four masts into which 16 survivors managed to scramble.

The distress rockets were answered by the Porthoustock lifeboat which first came upon an upturned ship's lifeboat (one of the two launched) and on turning it over found two ladies still alive. Shortly after, the Porthoustock lifeboat found the other ship's boat, water-logged and drifting helplessly with 22 survivors on board.

After landing the survivors, the lifeboat set out again and arriving on the scene of the disaster spent the rest of the night rescuing the 16 cold and desperate survivors from the masts in a perilous and exhausting operation.

On 18 October 1898, *Pulman's Weekly News* gave the following graphic account from one of the survivors, Steward F. Nicklen :

'The first indication of anything wrong came when all the passengers were at dinner. There was no panic. Everyone seemed resigned to their fate. Passengers were sitting down on the deck huddled together. Everybody did their duty and could do no more. By this time the ship had heeled over, and the water was level with the boat deck. We assisted in rescuing as many families as we possibly could and the children. There was a family of five, named Pemberton, and their maid, and we got them into the boat. Then we called for any more women or children, but they were on the other side. We cut all the boat lashings, as the ship was settling down. There were then about 20 passengers in the boat I was getting off.

'I jumped overboard, and struck out with a lifebelt on, and was dashed up against the ship's side between it and the lifeboat. I made a grab at the lifelines, hung on, and was pulled into the lifeboat. Two others jumped overboard, and were both of them picked up There were women and children in the boat. We had some difficulty in clearing the falls, but just managed to get them adrift, as the big ship was sinking. It was only just in time. The lifeboat was dashed twice against the ship's side, and half filled with water. We got the oars out and everyone who could pull, pulled for their lives. The rest took off their hats and jackets and started bailing out. We used everything we could to get the water out. After getting away from the sinking ship we kept head on to the wind to steer clear of the rocks. About a mile from the shore we could see the Manacles. It was dark but clear. In keeping the boat's head to the sea we pulled back to the wreckage three times. The vessel had settled right down, and we could hear cries for help, but we could give no help as we were three parts full of water.

'When the lifeboat from Porthoustock signalled we replied, and we were picked up by it, and all taken on board. On the way to Porthoustock we picked up a lady passenger who was crying for help. She turned out to be a Miss Noble, who had been in the water three and a half hours. I got her into the boat. When we landed there were 28 in the boat, independent of the crew.'

The total loss of life was 106 passengers and crew. Captain Griffiths and all his deck officers went down with the *Mohegan*. The Inquiry which followed never established why the *Mohegan* was so far off course, all who could have thrown light on the tragedy had perished.

Included on the list of those drowned was the name of twenty-four-years-old Nelson Yeaxlee, described as a baker on the ill-fated ship. He was the son of Mr Clarence Yeaxlee, who for some years had carried on a baker's and pastry cook's business in Middle Street and subsequently Earle Street, Yeovil. Nelson left a widow Kate, who as Kate Phillips he had married in St John's church, Yeovil on 5 April 1895 and a four-year-old son, Robert.

In St Keverne's churchyard on the Lizard Peninsular, over 40 victims of the tragedy were buried in a mass grave marked by a cross on the base on which is engraved the word MOHEGAN.

The Mohegan *wrecked on the Manacle Reef.*

A TURBULENT YEAR

1830 was a turbulent year in England. The scent of political and parliamentary reform was in the air and the Duke of Wellington voiced the fears of many when he said, 'Beginning reform is beginning revolution.' There was widespread discontent in the countryside and 'Captain Swing' and his men were burning hayricks and smashing the machines which were seen by many agricultural labourers to threaten their already meagre livelihoods. Poverty was grinding and widespread and it was reported in February 1830 that at 'Castle Cary the population is under 1900 and there are 1000 names on the poor book receiving more or less of Parish pay'.

1830 was a violent year in South Somerset. James Lane, a small farmer living at the aptly named 'Deadman's Post' in the parish of Buckland St Mary, was found guilty and transported to Australia for life for the manslaughter of his twelve-years-old son John. At Chard, John Russell was accused of killing Joan Turner and although found guilty of the capital crime of murder and sentenced to hang, the punishment was commuted to transportation for life to Australia.

During the late evening of 10 August, Mr Simeon Stucky, a substantial builder of Chard, disappeared as he rode on his horse Old Tom, home from Stratton, near South Petherton, but despite a wide-spread search, his severely battered body lay undiscovered for several weeks in a wheat field near Dinnington. There is an air of mystery surrounding the builder's violent end. He was not robbed of the money he was known to have been carrying and none of his personnel effects, including a fob watch, were taken. He had no known enemies, so why was he ambushed and beaten to death? Despite extensive enquiries and a number of suspects, the murderer or murders remain unknown to this day. There is, however, the suggestion that Mr Stucky's death was caused when for some reason his horse, had bolted and thrown its rider dragging him across the fields. Old Tom was found the following morning riderless on Chillington Common but we will never know what really happened during that August night nearly two hundred years ago.

Travelling along the narrow roads and lanes after dark could be a perilous undertaking as Mr Gilpin, a Crewkerne surgeon, discovered on a February evening returning from a visit to Martock. As the surgeon reached the Two Mile Stone on the Crewkerne road, he saw a shadowy figure detach itself from the darkness of the bushes and suddenly there was a flash, followed by a loud bang as a gun was fired straight at him. Mr Gilpin's head was jerked as his hat was blown away by the shot and then his horse bolted a full speed down the road to Crewkerne. No more shots followed and a few minutes later he caught up with a cart being driven by Mr Mills, a local baker, accompanied by a friend. The two men needed no persuasion to return with the surgeon to hunt down the would-be assassin, but by the time they arrived at the scene, the assailant had disappeared into the night. Mr Gilpin recovered his hat which showed what a lucky he had experienced. The ball had entered the hat just above the right side of his head and taking a slanting course had exited on the left side just under the crown; an inch lower and the surgeon would have been a dead man. On his arrival back at Crewkerne baker Mills told the authorities that as he passed the Two Mile Stone he had made out in the gloom, the figure of a tall man wearing light coloured clothes and who appeared to be hiding something under his arm. A reward of £100, equivalent to over four years wages for a farm labourer, was offered for the apprehension and conviction of the attacker but he was never found.

The following month, a Lieutenant Brown was robbed and severely injured near Stoke St Mary as he returned to Taunton. It was suggested that the Lieutenant had been mistaken for his brother who was also travelling along the same road carrying a large sum of money. The robbers were never caught

Towards the end of 1830, there was an outbreak of highway robberies around Chard, and during the evening of 15 December, Mr John Clinch was waylaid as he returned home to Chard from Taunton. Three men dragged him from his horse, he was beaten and robbed. However, Mr Clinch had recognised one of his assailants and all three were soon taken into custody. At the Somerset Assizes held in March 1831, two eighteen-year-olds, Richard Gough and Joseph Turner, and twenty-years-old John Berryman, were found guilty of robbing Mr John Clinch on the King's highway and sentenced to be transported to Australia for the rest of their natural lives. On 22 July 1831, Gough, Turner and Berryman left England together with 220 other felons on the convict ship *Strathfieldsaye*, arriving four months later on 15 November in Van Diemen's Land (Tasmania).

Richard Gough and Joseph Turner were sent to a prison hulk similar to the one shown here, to await transportation to Van Diemen's Land.

THE RECKLEFORD SCHOOL RIOT OF 1921

Mr John Reid, was the long-serving and popular headmaster of Reckleford School, and on his retirement after thirty-eight years service, the *Western Gazette* wrote on 21 January 1921, that:

'An interesting and unique event in the educational life of Yeovil took place on Wednesday afternoon, when Mr Jno. Reid, who for thirty-eight years has been the head-master of Reckleford Schools, entered upon well-merited retirement, and his long and valuable services were marked by several handsome presentations. Appointed head-master in 1883, Mr Reid has survived every member of the old School Board which appointed him, and has been responsible for the educational training of no fewer than 6,000 children. Amongst those gathered to bid him farewell were the Chairman (the Mayor) and members of the Yeovil Borough's Education Committee, head-masters, head-mistresses and teachers of other schools in the borough, and past teachers who had served under Mr Reid. The Mayor [Alderman W. R. E. Mitchelmore] paid a warm tribute to Mr Reid's long and faithful service, and he said that he felt gratified that his own sons were taught by such a head-master. His own feeling was that they were losing one who might be likened to a guiding star to the younger members of the Education Committee. Mr Reid was the oldest member of their staff, and on many occasions they had referred to his matured opinions on educational questions.'

Master Dick Waller, on behalf of the pupils, presented Mr Reid with a 'handsome ink-stand with cut glass bottles and silver fittings, and an album containing the names of the 133 young subscribers to the gift was also presented to the retiring head by Master Reginald Lacey.

Mr E. A. Stagg, the head assistant master and oldest member of the Reckleford School staff, presented Mr Reid with a 'handsome aneroid barometer in a carved fumed oak case, with silver face' on behalf of his colleagues and read letters of appreciation from former pupils, including one from the retiring headmaster's first pupil. More presentations and speeches followed and in thanking everyone for their generosity and friendship, Mr Reid concluded by saying that he would be sorry to see the Reckleford School ever disappear because with it would disappear the school's longstanding traditions.

This pleasant occasion, however, would trigger a chain of quite surprising events.

A few weeks later, in the morning of Monday 14 February, about 30 senior boys from Reckleford School marched noisily around the main streets bearing a placard announcing that they wanted Mr Stagg to be the new headmaster, and not the head appointed by the Education Committee from Southampton. Enquiries by the *Western Gazette* revealed that earlier that morning, some boys had come to school fully prepared to demonstrate, the word 'strike' had been scrawled on several walls, and during play-time, half the school had poured out into Reckleford shouting, chanting and 'demonstrating'. Mr Stagg, who was acting as headmaster,

THE RECKLEFORD SCHOOL RIOT OF 1921

got most of the youngsters back into school, but about 30 went off into town waving their placard. Back in school, the classes were given a 'talking to' by Mr Stagg, messages were sent to the truants ordering them to return, and a letter despatched to each parent asking them to send their son to school that afternoon. To no avail, and at two o'clock, a large number of boys assembled in Wyndham Fields, and about a hundred marched off behind their placards into town; none of the truants returned to school.

On hearing of this new turn of events, Mr Stagg went in search of the boys and finally caught up with them in Preston Grove where he halted the procession. After a considerable amount of persuasion, he marched the boys back to school where they were 'severely lectured'.

All the truants were back in school the following day, but the protest was not over, and a petition was drawn up signed by 70 boys for presentation to the mayor saying that if Mr Stagg was not made headmaster, they would go on strike on Monday 11 April, the day the new headmaster would take up office.

On Wednesday, a deputation of senior boys marched to the mayor's home and at his request, the youngsters told him that the school wanted Mr Stagg to be appointed headmaster in view of his long service. In reply, the mayor explained that the Education Committee had done what they considered was best for education and the pupils. He hoped they would act fairly with the new headmaster when he arrived in April, but in the meantime, he would bring the matter before the Education Committee.

On 14 February 1921 the Reckleford school boys paraded Yeovil's main streets, including the Borough shown here.

However, from the following stern and forthright letter written by the mayor to the Reckleford School boys, it seems that the agitation had not died down:

'BOYS – I am surprised to learn after our interview on Wednesday last you are continuing the agitation on the question of the Headship of the School. My purpose in talking to you was to reason you into obedience, instead of getting you caned into submission. It is a pity for you to misunderstand. I took what you had done on the day you left the school during school hours to be only a generous boyish impulse, but from information to hand it is clear that it was not so. Other persons are evidently more responsible than yourselves. If this foolishness does not stop, exposure will follow.

'The Education Authority knows its powers and its responsibility. The duty of parents, the position of the teachers, and the obedience of the children is all clearly laid down in the Education Act as applying the Local Authorities. If the law which compels you to attend school is again broken, the Education Committee will certainly act swift and severe.'

It would appear that the mayor's warning had its effect and there were no further reports of 'rebellion', but some few years later, Mr A. E. Stagg was appointed Headmaster of Reckleford School.

A DAY AT THE SOMERSET WINTER ASSIZES

A brief look at some of the serious cases which were brought before the judge Mr Justice Mellor at the Somerset Winter Assizes, held at Taunton on 9 December 1867, and reported in the *Western Flying Post* on the following Friday, the 13th:

The first to be heard was the case of Mary Jane Palmer an eighteen-years-old servant who pleaded guilty to 'endeavouring to conceal the birth of her male child by attempting to destroy the body in a fire at Winscombe'.

The medical evidence suggested that the baby had not been born alive, and the judge, bearing in mind that Mary Jane had been in custody since the last August, sentenced her to four months hard labour.

Two Taunton men, seventeen-years-old, John Goodman ominously described as 'a striker' and eighteen-years-old blacksmith, Abraham Richards, pleaded not guilty to stealing a coat from George Billett in the town on 23 November.

The prosecution's case was that during the evening in question, George Billett was walking in East Reach carrying the new coat he had recently purchased when he was grabbed and held fast from behind by Goodman, whilst Richards 'smashed his face'. Following a short struggle, the coat was dropped, he saw Goodman pick it up and both had run-off. However, the two young men were soon arrested and placed in the same cell at Taunton police station. The court was told that the evidence against Richards was a conversation between the two overhead by Police Constable Dewey 'which clearly showed that the persons were mates'. Goodman was found guilty and sentenced to eighteen months hard labour, but for some reason, the evidence against Richards was not sufficient to prove his guilt and he was acquitted.

Described as 'a sturdy railway navvy', Joseph Webb appeared charged with the manslaughter of his wife Susan at Yatton on the previous 23 September. Protesting 'I am innocent, I couldn't help it', he pleaded not guilty.

The prosecution alleged that on the night of the 23 September, the couple had been drinking 'pretty freely' in several local public houses and were on their way home when according to the prisoner's account his wife had one of her epileptic fits outside the house of a Mr Green. However, Mr Green's testimony challenged that of the prisoner and the witnessed stated that he had heard the sounds of a struggle and blows.

The medical evidence was given by a well-known local surgeon, Mr Horace Swete, who told the court that 'some of the symptoms of violent epilepsy were wanting, and that the effusion of blood, which was the cause of death must have been caused by some violence-a-succession of blows-leaving it an open question, whether it was occasioned by falls in the struggle or blows or kicks.'

In his defence, Joseph Webb told the court that he could not have caused his wife's death by kicking because he was wearing 'thin boots'. He went on to say that he had done all he could and his mistake had been to trying to get Susan out of the road, and the struggle this had involved rather than holding her down where she had fallen.

Following the judge's summing up with the *Western Flying Post* reported was 'decidedly in the prisoner's favour' the jury acquitted thirty-three-years-old Joseph Webb.

A fight in a Bath public house ended in the death of one of the contestants and a forty-years-old labourer, James Bell found himself facing Mr Justice Mellor at the Winter Assizes charged with the manslaughter of James Goney at the Rising Sun on Grove Street on 3 September.

The court was told that James Bell had gone into the Rising Sun for a drink on the evening of 3 September, when James Goney had provoked him by pulling his hat down over his eyes, and following the prisoner's protests had struck him several times. Following more provocation and attacks, the prisoner had drawn his pocket knife and stabbed the deceased in the stomach.

At the time the wound had not seemed serious and James Goney had left the public house but later that evening he had been taken ill and died in hospital the following day from internal bleeding.

The jury found James Bell guilty of manslaughter but recommended him for mercy on account of the provocation he had received from the deceased and he was sentenced to nine months imprisonment.

Frederick Hunt was sentenced to twelve years penal servitude for 'endeavouring to discharge a loaded firearm at Joseph Chamberlain while in execution of his duty with intent to commit murder at Nailsea' on 20 October 1867.

Frederick Hunt described as a labourer was charged with 'endeavouring to discharge a loaded pistol at Joseph Chamberlain while in the execution of his duty with intent to commit murder at Nailsea on 20 October last'.

The prosecution's case was that on the night of 20 October, two police constables Chamberlain and Chambers had arrested a man named Pullin for stealing cabbages and were about to take him into the police station when a number of men rushed the officers and tried to free Pullin. In the struggle which followed Constable Chamberlain was set upon by Hunt but as the two wrestled on the ground, Hunt had pulled out a pistol, pressed it against the constable's chest and squeezed the trigger. Fortunately for the officer and Hunt, the pistol did not fire, because if it had not only would Constable Chamberlain have been seriously, if not fatally wounded, but Frederick Hunt could have been facing the gallows.

The prisoner's defence was that the constables were the aggressors and were acting unlawfully and he was defending himself, but this did not dissuade the jury from finding him guilty and the *Western Flying Post* recorded that 'It having been shown that the prisoner had been sentenced in 1857 to six years penal servitude for burglary, he was now sentenced to twelve years' penal servitude.'

Of all the cases tried at the Winter Assizes of 1867, possibly the most tragic was that of a forty-six-years-old labourer, Richard Barrow who appeared charged with the manslaughter of his daughter Elizabeth on 3 September at his lodgings on Milk Street, Bath,

The court was told that since his wife's death in the previous May, the prisoner had been drinking heavily and had subsequently neglected his two daughters, one aged four and Elizabeth aged eighteen months. Barrow was said to be earning 12 shillings a week which it was considered to be sufficient to support his daughters.

Mr Montague, an inspector of nuisances, testified that in the course of his duties he had visited the prisoner's lodgings and found the child lying dead on a box in a rapid state of decomposition and with its eyes open 'showing that no one had been present at her death'.

A postmortem examination carried out by Mr Gulliford Hopkins of the Bath Infirmary on the badly decomposed body of little Elizabeth and he was of the opinion that the child had died of starvation.

Richard Barrow's plea of not guilty was dismissed by the jury who found him guilty and the judge sentenced him to six months imprisonment with hard labour.

The conviction of a sixteen-years-old labourer for attempting 'to commit a nameless offence' and a sentence of fifteen months' hard labour concluded the Somerset Winter Assizes of 1867.

'LAWRENCE OF THE RAF'

It may come as a surprise to readers that during the Second World War (1939-1945) a Somerset-born man became known as the 'Lawrence of the RAF' named after the famous Lawrence of Arabia. On the 20 April 1945, the following article appeared in the columns of the *Western Gazette*:

'BARNARDO BOY HERO – YEOVIL BORN OFFICER'S EXPLOITS
A remarkable story was told in the "Sunday Pictorial" of a young man stated to have been born in Yeovil, Somerset who has become one of the heroes of the war and one of the most romantic figures in the Royal Air Force.

It is recorded that at the tender age of three months a baby boy wrapped in a shawl was taken late one night to Dr. Barnardo's Home in Essex. That was nearly 31 years ago. The Home gave the little bundle a name and christened him "Jack Churchill."

Today he is Flying Officer Jack Churchill, D.S.O., D.F.C. of the R.A.F.V.R.

"LAWRENCE OF THE R.A.F."
Because of his secret flights into the heart of Burma he has come to be known throughout South-East Asia Command as the "Lawrence of the R.A.F." Time and time again he has risked death over the steaming jungle, always to come through smiling and successful. At present his exploits cannot be told. On each occasion he has received a decoration he had been flying hazardous missions in Burma. He is the only man in South-East Asia Command to have flown more than 30,000 miles.

But not all his life has Flying Officer Jack Churchill known success. Capt. Lewin, the Governor of the Dr. Barnardo's Boys' Garden City said of him: "To us he was always a bit of a problem child---an individualist. Not much of a boy for study, but brilliant at sport and as tough as they came. Even to-day, although since I must have had thousands of boys through the school, young Jack still stands out sharply in my memory."

In civilian life it is recorded that he never found a job he really liked and never one he could keep. For years in lived in Wardour-street, London. Young Cyril and Fred Weaver, two young Londoners, of Burgess-road, East Ham, came to know him at that time. One day the two Weaver sons told their parents of the hard life of their new-found "orphan" friend. "Could we find a room for him in our home?" asked young Fred. The room was found, and for the first time young Churchill found his first real "mother and father."

"NEW JACK CHURCHILL"
Then one of the Weavers' sons, Fred, was captured by the Japanese at Singapore. From that day onwards it was if a new Jack Churchill was born. Mr. Weaver said, " Somehow,' he told us. 'I'll get the chance to avenge Freddie,' " In rapid succession, he was promoted Sergeant

'The boys' Garden City where Jack Churchill spent his boyhood.

>   Pilot, was granted a commission, won the D.S.O. and the D.F.C. Yet it is recorded of him that he was too shy to go to a dance and too nervous to learn to drive a car.'

And so what more can be found out about Jack Churchill, the 'Lawrence of the RAF'. In 1944 and 1945 when Jack was flying the hazardous missions, we were fighting the Japanese in a savage war in Burma and should you come down in the jungle and be captured by the Japanese you could be killed on the spot or sent to one of the notorious prison camps where your chances of survival could be small.

Jack was indeed born in Yeovil, on 16 June 1914 to be precise, and named Jack Churchill on the birth certificate issued by Mr James Golledge, the Registrar for the Yeovil Registration District. Therefore Jack was already named when he was taken some three months later to the Dr Barnardo's Home.

Jack Churchill was flying in the Far East, initially with the RAF's No 1576 (Special Duties) Flight and then with No 357 Squadron, supplying the Allied ground forces operating behind the Japanese lines in Burma and subsequently in Malaya. The units were equipped with a variety of aircraft, including some Yeovil built Westland Lysanders.

Jack's exploits resulted in his being awarded the Distinguished Flying Cross (DFC) in February 1944 for:

'Completing many sorties, involving long-distance flights over difficult terrain, often in adverse weather. He has at all times displayed outstanding devotion to duty and his example of courage, skill and fortitude has been highly commendable.'

In March 1945, whilst serving with No 357 Squadron in the junior rank of Flying Officer he was awarded the Distinguished Service Order (DSO) for completing:

'A large number of sorties, involving long flights over Burma. He has consistently displayed the highest standard of devotion to duty and his example has been most impressive. In January 1945, Flying Officer Churchill was the pilot and captain in an aircraft detailed for a sortie. The operation called for a high degree of skill and resolution. That success was achieved on a flight covering some thousands of miles in all is a fine tribute to this officer's superb airmanship, great captaincy and iron determination.'

The sortie referred to in the citation was taken on 25 January 1945 and involved a non-stop round-trip of 3700 miles lasting twenty-one hours fifty-five minutes in a Liberator four-engine bomber and until then was the furthest and longest supply operation flown over enemy territory in the South-East Asia Command. Some years later it was revealed by a member of the crew that on the return landing there was petrol left for only twenty minutes flying time.

Jack was promoted to the rank of Flight Lieutenant in July 1945 but bearing in mind the many dangerous missions he flew, the award of the prestigious DSO and DFC, and being given the title of 'Lawrence of the RAF', Jack Churchill seems to have disappeared from public attention.

And by the way, it seems that Fred Weaver survived the war and his capture by the Japanese.

THIEVES AND QUARRELS

The meeting of the Bath and West of England Society, or as we know it today, the Bath and West Show, was held in Yeovil during the first week of June 1856 at Ram Park – now Sidney Gardens, and surrounding area. Besides the thousands of visitors, who would come to marvel at the displays of modern machinery, to admire the livestock and enjoy the entertainments at the three-day show, there were a few whose interests were less innocent.

Whenever, or wherever, large crowds gather, certain members of the criminal fraternity are never far away, and the Bath and West of England Society's Show was no exception. The attraction of easy pickings was bound to lure a few felons to the town, but some were in for a big surprise.

The *Western Flying Post* reported that the police arrangements were excellent and officers from the Bath, Bristol and Exeter police, under the supervision of Superintendent Hughes of Bath, were in Yeovil to assist the town force in crime prevention 1856 style. Three well-known thieves were quickly recognised in the town before they could get to the showground and taken into custody, two more were arrested on their arrival at the Hendford Railway Station and another two picked up at the show. According to the *Flying Post*, the arrests were merely precautionary, the principle being acted upon was that prevention was better than cure, and commented dryly, that 'No doubt it was better for the thieves themselves as well as the honest and liege subjects of Her Majesty, that they should be in the lock-up than allowed to indulge in the practice of plunder.' The newspaper went on to tell how one of the villains had 'Expressed a wish at the station-house that they had been allowed only half an hour to operate in.'

On Saturday 7 June, the day following the end of the show, the seven unnamed individuals appeared before the Borough Magistrates on suspicion of being thieves. Superintendent Hughes told the Bench that he was pressing no charges but stated that he had known a gang of pick-pockets come to Bath and within half an hour had carried off £36. He also expressed his great satisfaction work of the superintendent and officers of the Yeovil police and the special constables.

The magistrates discharged the seven, they were taken to the railway station under police escort and sent packing out of town on the next train.

The *Western Flying Post* commented that it was pleasing to note 'That the utmost good order prevailed in the town during the entire week, a circumstance which is all creditable to the inhabitants and the many thousands of strangers who thronged the streets.'

Not so peaceful were Susan Seymour and Hannah Best, who were brought before the same Bench on 7 June, charged with making a disturbance and fighting the previous evening. They were cautioned and discharged.

One villain who had not been recognised by the police was Hannah Brown from Bristol, who told the magistrates 'that she had come to Yeovil in search of

Some forty years later Sidney Gardens was laid out on a large part of Ram Park where the Bath and West Show was held in 1856.

her husband', but was charged with picking the pocket of one Henry Dyke. The Bench was told by Henry Dyke that he had met the prisoner at the gateway to the Red Lion Inn at Kingston, but after they had walked a little way into town, she had removed his purse from his pocket, extracted several shillings and replaced it. In her defence, Hannah Brown asked to be allowed the benefit of the doubt, and revealed that she had been transported to Australia for twenty-one years for 'selling whiskey without a license'. However, the magistrates concluded that this was an unlikely tale, as the offence was not one for which the sentence of transportation applied and sent Hannah Brown down for three months' hard labour.

Also on 7 June, Robert Slade appeared charged by an unnamed lady street stall-keeper with injuring some articles on her stand, and applying for him to be bound over to keep the peace. It transpired, however, that Robert Slade and the lady concerned had lived together as man and wife, but had separated in January last. On Friday 6 June, she had a toy stall in the town and the defendant had come up and broken one of the dolls. In his defence, Robert Slade stated that the article was his because the lady had been accustomed to taking his goods and selling them. The magistrates dismissed the case.

THE MISSING BALLOT PAPERS

In 1894, Parish Councils were established, and in December of that year, the first elections were held. Urban and Rural District Councils were also established, but these authorities were disbanded and their areas merged into the new District Councils eighty years later in 1974; Parish Councils are still with us.

In the Langport area, where there were elections for the new Langport Rural District Council and a number of new Parish Councils, every Returning Officer's nightmare happened, as related in the *Pulman's Weekly News* on 18 December 1894.

Bow Street Langport at the time the ballot papers went missing in the local elections in 1894.

'When the rural electors of more than seven parishes presented themselves at the places prepared for recording their votes for their selected candidates under the Parish and District Councils Act, great was their disappointment when they were informed that the primary essential for the *modus operandi* – the ballot papers – were not forthcoming, and that they were perforce obliged to go home without exercising their much talked of privilege. In seven parishes excited electors were rushing to and fro with wonderment depicted upon their visages, and reiterating the question to each other "Why can't we vote?" to receive the reply "The ballot papers baint come." And then the look of wonderment became intensified. Said one man to another, as the pair were plodding homeward to an outlying part of Huish Episcopi, "This be a nice game a dragging I in here on a fule's errand; I baint a-comin' in agin, I can tell 'ee. Paarish Councils! Haw! We' got'un Councils anuff already! What be the gude o' they to I!"

'The various candidates and their friends were equally excited and bewildered. Everything for properly carrying out the elections was in a state of preparedness, but when the time arrived for opening the polling places to the electors there were no ballot papers – they had not arrived, but were expected by the next train. In Langport at the Board Schools, where the balloting for Langport and Huish Episcopi was to take place, a notice was posted delaying the opening for a couple of hours, but on electors again presenting themselves, the rooms were in readiness, but there were no officials and no ballot papers. They had not come. There was, therefore, no other resources but to leave the decision of the momentous question as to which of the candidates should have a seat on the first Parish or District Council, as the case may be, until some future date.

'Upon no-one does the disappointment caused by the singular failure fall more heavily than on the Returning Officer (Mr E. Q. Louch), who had devoted a considerable amount of time and undoubted ability in mastering the details and explaining the Act to the parishioners, and had, he thought, done everything that devolved upon him for the successful fulfilment of his functions. With the idea of securing uniformity in the ballot papers, he entrusted the order for printing them to a London firm of Local Government Board printers. As they did not arrive when they were expected, enquiries were made by telegraph, and at 10a.m. on Saturday he received a telegram from the printers to the effect that they had been despatched early that morning and were *en route* by passenger train. But as they had not arrived by two o'clock (when polling was due to start) it became impossible to proceed with the election that day, and there was no other resource but to awaited the decision of the County Council or the Local Government Board as to what course must be taken in the case of such a remarkable failure. A large number of candidates interviewed the Returning Officer, who candidly acknowledged his responsibility, and unfeignedly regretted the unfortunate occurrence.

'The parishes affected by the non-delivery of the papers were:-Langport, Huish Episcopi and Kingsbury Episcopi, for Parish Councillors; Aller and Long Sutton, for District Councillors; and Curry Rivel and Somerton for both Parish and District Councillors. In Langport and Somerton considerable excitement prevailed. Addresses were published by the numerous candidates, and the towns were flooded with literature posted on walls. There was every appearance of close contests for the coveted seats.

'The missing ballot papers turned up by the last train on Saturday night, and it was stated that they were entrained at Paddington at three p.m. The cause of their not arriving at Langport at the proper time is still open to conjecture.'

BRIEFLY SHOCKING AND SURPRISING

Bath
'By a Letter from Bath we hear, that on the 9th instant a melancholy Accident happened to Mr William Chapman, Saddler, one of the Common-Council-Men of that City, as follows: Mr. Chapman having bought a Case of Pistols of a Gentleman lodging at Mr Gill's, a Pastry-Cook in Westgate-street, went afterwards with them to Mr Gill's Room, and drank some Coffee with him; and laying the Pistols down, Mr Gill took one of them up, and not imagining t'was charged, cock'd and snapt it; the Pistol went off, and the Ball entering Mr Chapman's left Side penetrated thro' his Body, and came out at his right Breast; whereupon he ran out into the Street, crying he was a dead Man, and had gone but a few Yards before he dropped down dead. The Coroner's Jury sat on his Body, and brought in their Verdict Accidental Death.'
The Sherborne Mercury and Weekly Advertiser, 22 February 1737.

Bridgwater
'The brig, *St. Pierre,* of Bridgwater, Mr Pulman, owner, in going down the River Parrett, on Monday se'nnight, from the darkness of the night, ran on a sand bank, and was capsized. The tide in the morning, broke over her, and reduced her to a wreck, by which all on board were drowned, except the Captain, who floated ashore, on one of the hatchways, and another man named Rossitor. The crew consisted of two seamen, the pilot, the Captain and his son. An aged female who had her passage to Newport, to which port the brig was bound, was also among the persons lost. Both seamen, who perished, had families, and one of them nine children.'
The Taunton Courier, 18 December 1844.

Chard
'The accompanying original photograph was taken by John Stringfellow (the inventor of the first aeroplane) by means of one of the earliest forms of plate photography, and is one of the few photographs of an actual gallows tree. The tree itself had been a mighty specimen, several of its largest branches, even larger than those shown ran for more than 40 feet almost horizontally from the fork and it was on these limbs that the executions in connection with the Monmouth Rebellion were carried in almost all their incredible crudeness and barbarity. Twelve Chard men were hung at Dorchester, but twelve others were sent to be hanged on this tree at

John Stringfellow's early photograph of the Gallows Tree.

131

Chard. Amongst these were William Williams, the Duke's own body servant and James Durnett, reputed to be John Bunyan's son-in-law.

The old tree was cut down to allow for a road diversion over a railway bridge when the Southern system was first connected up with Chard.'

The Somerset Year Book, 1931.

Shepton Mallet
'On Sunday morning last February 18th, a prisoner named James made an ingenious and daring escape from the County Gaol here. At about seven o'clock as the town postman was proceeding to the Town Office he observed a rope hanging from a wall adjoining the trial corridor of the prison, and immediately gave an alarm.

The Governor rushed out only partly dressed to see the mode in which the prisoner escaped. It appears that every evening the prisoners have to tie up their clothes and give them to the guard whose duty is to have their cells properly locked up for the night, but instead of so doing the prisoner gave up a bolster or some other article of clothing and remained in his trousers and waistcoat. No suspicions were aroused as the guard did not examine the contents and in the night when all appeared to be asleep the prisoner by some means made a hole through the roof and then fastened a long cord of slip and cocoa matting got down the boundary wall, a height of some 30 feet, and made his escape. The guards and other men were sent in every direction and between 11 and 12 o'clock the fugitive was captured near Frome, having walked whole distance, bare footed. He was immediately brought back securely handcuffed and safely lodged in a stronger cell for the future.'

The Western Flying Post, 27 February 1866.

Over three years later:

'Between 11 and 12 o'clock on Wednesday a heavy storm of rain and wind visited this town blowing down several chimneys and many chimney pots. Several windows were blown out of various houses, one of which has not yet been found. Many trees were blown down near the town; but the greatest misfortune for the younger people is the damage done to the well-known "Kiss-tree" the overspreading branches of which, it is feared, will afford shelter no more.'

Western Gazette, 21 October 1870.

South Petherton
The Yeovil Rural District Council at its meeting in June 1908, received a letter from Admiral Baker complaining of the nuisance from the stench of pigs kept by some of his neighbours. The Admiral wrote that although Mr Fish, the inspector of nuisances, had agreed on several occasions that his complaint was not exaggerated, the official appeared unwilling or unable to get the nuisance abated. This lack of action had caused the Admiral to write to the council and with the onset of the hot weather, he was concerned at the possibility of an epidemic illness. He went on

to write that the council appeared to have done nothing to deal with the problem and if the Inspector was unable to cope with the nuisance then the matter should be referred to the council's medical officer of health.

Replying to a question from Colonel H. E. Harbin, the chairman of the council, Mr Fish confirmed that there was an occasional smell when the wind was in a certain direction, but it was a matter of opinion whether this amounted to a nuisance.

Colonel Blake opined that this might be a nuisance at one time and not at another. However, he thought the medical officer of health should visit the area and see whether it was a permanent danger to the health of the residents.

The Reverend Armstrong suggested that the inspector of nuisances was showing a greater laxity to the nearness of pig styes to dwelling houses than his predecessor had.

Mr J. G. Vaux observed that there had been no complaints before Admiral Baker came to live here and this opened up a wide question as the pig styes had been there for generations and they were from 100 to 200 yards away from the Admiral's house.

The council referred the complaint to the medical officer of health and the Works Committee were instructed to visit South Petherton and report back.

It seems that the problem was cleared up to everyone's satisfaction because a few months later the Admiral wrote thanking the council for the action they had taken to abate the nuisance.

Western Gazette, June 1908.

Wells

'A party of strolling fellows, with which the country is at present infested, five in number visited Mr Robert Teek, at Hill-house farm, about two miles from Wells, under the pretence of vending envelopes and other wares; and not plying their trade to their satisfaction, they walked uninvited into his garden and commenced depredation on his fruit. Mr Teek, with laudable courage, attacked them, and after a severe struggle, secured two of them, and, aided by one of his men, attempted to bring them to the prison at Wells. The way lies across the fields, and is lonely; about midway, the three who had escaped came up with them and, armed with sticks, attempted a rescue. Mr Teek, who is a resolute and athletic person, and who was also now provided with staves, boldly resisted them, and after a profusion of hard blows on either side, he again succeeded in driving off the three and proceeded with the two on his way to Wells; on his way up the High-street, he was again overtaken and attacked by these men, but this time there was no lack of assistance, and his prisoners were safely lodged in the gaol and shortly afterwards a third was apprehended in the town; the two others have escaped The case was heard before the county magistrates the following morning, and the prisoners were summarily convicted. The most desperate of them was sentenced to six months' hard labour, and the other two to two months' each.'

Taunton Courier, 30 August 1848.

CAPTAIN HUNT GOES ON THE RUN

In March 1655, a minor rebellion led by a veteran Royalist, John Penruddock, broke out against the Commonwealth of Oliver Cromwell. After occupying Salisbury, breaking open the gaol and releasing all the prisoners, the 300 rebels marched to Blandford where they proclaimed Charles II, King of England. Unfortunately for the rebels, the good folk of Dorset wanted nothing of this rebellion as the memories of the late Civil War were still fresh in their minds, and Penruddock and his little army retreated west through Yeovil and Chard until they were routed in a bloodless skirmish at South Molton. John Penruddock was captured with some of his followers and was executed at Exeter on 16 May 1655. Another rebel officer, Captain Thomas Hunt, was sentenced to death by beheading at Ilchester Gaol where he was given into the care of the Sheriff of Somerset his namesake, but no relation, Robert Hunt whose home was the Manor of Compton Pauncefoot.

Captain Hunt's execution was fixed for the evening of 7 May, but the axe needed to remove his head was proving difficult to find. It had to have a blade of 11 inches to carry out the task, and implements of this size were not in plentiful supply. The problem in procuring the axe, and the time required to build the scaffold before the Shire Hall in the market place at Ilchester, had now delayed the execution until Thursday 10 May.

On Wednesday night, the eve of the execution, Captain Hunt was allowed a last visit from his two sisters, Marjorie and Elizabeth. They arrived at the gaol

Robert Hunt, Sheriff of Somerset was buried in the parish church of St Mary the Virgin, Compton Pauncefoot.

at about 10 o'clock and were shown to their brother's cell which he shared with two other prisoners. His two companions were absent during the visit, and alone with his sisters, a daring escape was put in hand. Captain Hunt quickly changed clothes with Marjorie, and then with Elizabeth went through the gaol, passing three doorkeepers and the main gate guard, to freedom. Back in the cell, Marjorie placed her brother's cloak and hat on a chair and got into his bed. On their return, the captain's cellmates thought he was asleep and took to their beds.

Having parted from his sister, Captain Hunt found himself wandering alone in the vicinity of Ilchester as dawn broke but without any idea of where he was; he could also hear the great bell of the gaol begin to toll for his impending execution. Just as he began to lose hope of making an escape, the captain espied a collier coming along the road leading a packhorse loaded with coal. Still in female disguise, Captain Hunt hailed the collier and in the conversation which followed discovered his destination. Telling the collier that he was travelling in the same direction, 'the lady' managed to persuade him to allow 'her' to ride with the coal on the horse. During the journey, the collier's Royalist sympathies soon became apparent and the captain took a desperate chance and disclosed that he was an escaped rebel. As events proved, this chance encounter was to save Captain Hunt's life, and in company with his newfound saviour, he rode across country to the collier's home on the edge of the lonely Somerset Levels.

The escape had now been discovered, Marjorie was arrested and confessed. Sister Elizabeth was also apprehended, and both ladies were lodged in Ilchester Gaol, where they remained without being brought to trial until their release two years later in 1657. On discovering Captain Hunt's escape the hue and cry was raised, and Parliamentary troops stationed in Ilchester were soon scouring the countryside. When he reached his home, the collier barricaded the door, no lights were lit, and the two men took cover in a small upper chamber of the cottage, each with a loaded musket preparing to sell their lives dearly if discovered. Before long a sheriff's officer with a troop of mounted men clattered into the yard and hammering on the door demanded entrance. At first, the collier and his wife made no sign, but as the shouting of the troopers became more threatening, the collier put his head out of the chamber window as if disturbed from sleep and demanded an explanation for this uproar. The sheriff's officer bellowed that the party was in pursuit of a prisoner escaped from Ilchester Gaol disguised as a female, and as he had orders to search every house, his men would force their way in if necessary. The collier replied that he would open the door as soon as he could get a light, but pretended that he had lost the steel for the tinder box. As no one else had any means of producing light, the troopers were told that they must search the house in the dark. The sheriff's officer by now had lost his patience with the apparent ignorance of the collier, and calling out that it was useless to waste time here because the stupid fellow did not know his right hand from his left, away galloped the party to the inexpressible relief of the fugitive and his faithful friends.

Captain Hunt remained hidden in the collier's cottage, and when the hue and cry had calmed down, the collier helped him in his escape to France where he joined the exiled Charles II and with whom he remained until returning to England at the Restoration some five years later. The name of the collier who saved the captain's life, and whether he was rewarded for the terrible risk he took for a stranger, remains one of history's secrets.

As for Sheriff Robert Hunt, the escape of his namesake was an obvious embarrassment, but it did not affect the career of this widely respected man. He continued in the office of Sheriff of Somerset for another year, served the County and Ilchester in the Parliaments of 1659 and 1660, and for the last two decades of his life continued to play an active role in County government as a Magistrate and Deputy Lieutenant. Robert Hunt now lies with his kin in the church of St Mary the Virgin in the peaceful village of Compton Pauncefoot.

DEATH IN THE COAL PIT

Driving through the rural parts of northern Somerset it is almost impossible to envisage those days when the area was a hive of activity – the Somerset Coalfields.

Coal mining was by its very nature was, and remains, very dangerous work, even in the best-regulated mine, disaster still lurks. Whilst there were many improvements in working the coal mines during the nineteenth century, fatal accidents remained a peril to be faced by men (boys and, in the early decades, women) as they toiled away in the dark hundreds of feet below ground.

The Somerset Coalfields closed in 1973 and during the following years, the scars of the industrial past have melted into the rural landscape.

During the eighteenth and early decades of the nineteenth centuries, the 'hooker system' was commonly used to raise and lower miners down hundreds of feet of a narrow shaft, rarely more than 4 feet wide, to the coal workings. By this means a number of miners sat or stood on loops of rope which they had hooked on to the end of the winding rope or on to a chain attached the to the rope. The men would then be lowered or raised up the shaft, sometimes with young boys sitting on their laps, holding on to the rope with one hand and fending off the sides of the narrow shaft with the other. This was the reality of hundreds of miners' lives and no matter how many times they had attached themselves to the winding rope, there must have been the fear lurking in the recesses of their minds, will the rope break!

Miraculously, such accidents were rare, but when one happened the news would travel around the coalfield and perhaps for a short while the daily journey up and down the shaft could be a nightmare.

Paulton Engine Coal Pit

The hooker system was used at the Paulton Engine Coal Pit when at about three o'clock on Friday afternoon, 26 March 1830, seven men and two boys assembled at the bottom of the shaft and 'hooked on' to the winding rope. The signal was given to wind them up the 600 feet to the surface through a narrow 3 feet wide shaft. The winding wheel of the steam engine (after which the pit was named), was engaged and began to haul up the thick flat hemp rope with its human cargo. Suddenly, the winding rope broke and seven men and two boys hurtled some 150 feet back down to the bottom followed by several hundred feet of heavy hemp rope said to have weighed over two tons. The fear of the rope breaking had become a reality that Friday afternoon, four men and one boy died instantly but by a miracle four survived but with terrible injuries.

During the five hours which followed, a new rope was attached to the engine, and the dead and injured brought to the surface. The news had quickly spread through Paulton and the men's relations rushed to the pit where the *Bath Chronicle* reported on 1 April that 'It is impossible to describe the agony of feeling expressed by the wives and children of the persons working at the pit during the time which elapsed from the breaking of the rope and a new one could be affixed, to bring up the dead and mutilated bodies of those who had fallen.'

The dead were named as forty-eight-years-old George Winter, who left a widow and five children, George Gregory thirty-eight, leaving a widow and six children, George Bull, twenty-four-years-old leaving a wife and one child, John Gregor twenty-five, left a wife, and the dead boy was fifteen-years-old John Bailey.

The four survivors were terribly injured, two with multiple compound fractures of the legs and there were fears that none would survive, but on this, the record appears to have remained silent.

On 5 April 1830, the *Sherborne Mercury* reported the accident and wrote that 'Only the day before a large party of the respectable inhabitants of the neighbourhood had decided on a descent to the bottom. They must shudder when they think of the dangerous risk of such an enterprise.'

The inquest which followed into the deaths of the miners heard that the winding rope had parted at one of the joints near the mouth of the shaft and had been examined only 'a few days previously and pronounced fit for twelve months'. A verdict of accidental death was returned.

The *Sherborne Mercury's* edition of 12 April recorded that at least 3000 people attended the funeral of the five miners at Paulton on the sixth of the month.

Hayeswood Coal Works, Timsbury.

One of the many dangers facing miners in the Somerset Coalfields was flooding, some from the natural water table and occasionally from nearby old abandoned workings. Hayeswood coal works adjoined some old workings but as they were in different ownership their exact location and condition were not known.

On Tuesday morning 4 February 1845 at about five o'clock, 100 men and boys descended the 1000 feet into the mine and dispersed to the several working faces some of which were almost a mile from the shaft. Accompanying the shift was Mr Evans, the works' overseer, and his attention was drawn to the unusual taste of some brackish tasting water collected by one of the overlookers of the previous night's shift. Mr Evans was not unduly concerned as he believed the water to be what was known as the 'bleeding of the coals' and which contained various minerals. However, the overlooker told Mr Evans that the singing sound normally accompanying the 'weeping' was unusually absent on this occasion. Having examined the place from which the water came, the works' overseer, concluded that there was no danger and proceeded into the workings on his daily duties.

Suddenly there was a violent gust of wind which nearly blew out the candle he was carrying followed immediately by the appearance in the dim light of a boy running for his life shouting that there was foul air and water pouring into the mine. It was reported in the *Bath Chronicle* that as the news of the incoming water reached the miners and their candles began to be blown out by the foul air pushed forward by the inundation, they frantically groped their way in the darkness to the bottom of the shaft in order to be drawn up into the fresh air.

Amongst the miners making their desperate way to the shaft, was Mr Evans who would later recall that he believed this took him over half an hour and that he had been in a fainting condition on his arrival. As the miners waited below the air was becoming 'more and more impure' and their feeling of desperation was becoming acute when it was realized that their only means of escape was the box used to haul coal up the shaft. The box could hold no more than 14 men at a time and when they realized this 'the greatest terror seized upon them'. However, some order prevailed and slowly the rescue was achieved but it was only just in time because the last miners to be drawn up were standing in water up to their shoulders as they clambered aboard the box.

A roll call of the rescued men found that 11 men and boys were missing and the search for survivors was hampered by the flooding and finally all hope was given up. The water in the mine was lowered over the succeeding months and some of the bodies of the missing miners were recovered.

New Rock Colliery, Radstock.

Unlike many of the United Kingdom's coalfields, the Somerset workings were generally free from explosive gases and the main source of miners' lights were candles. This did not mean that explosions did not occur but the human hand was evident in most cases.

On 7 February 1893, thirty-six-years-old, experience miner, Edward Emery, in company with brothers Edward and Isaac Targett, was filling eight lengths of thatching straws with gun powder for use as fuses.

A view of Radstock where Edmund Emery lost his life from the explosion in the New Rock Colliery.

Edward was an experienced shot firer using explosives to loosen the coal faces and the straw fuses would be inserted in the explosive charges.

The three men were sitting in an alcove near the upcast shaft where Edward had started taking a small quantity of powder from a powder box containing some three and a half pounds of explosive and carefully pouring it down into the narrow straw. Lighting for this operation was from Edward Emery's candle stuck on the wall of the alcove and two candles in holders at the back of the Targett brothers.

Edward Emery had just finished filling the last of the eight straws and pinched out his candle. Suddenly there was a violent explosion, one side of the powder box was blown away and hit Isaac Targett's face, taking away some skin, but Edward Emery's waistcoat and shirt were engulfed in a mass of flames. His namesake, Edward Targett managed to tear off the burning clothes but was slightly burnt in the process. The badly burned miner was taken home but died on 7 February from pneumonia and 'ulceration of the bowels' brought on by his injuries. Isaac Targett recovered from his injury.

The inquest into Edward Emery's death, failed to identify with any certainty the cause of the explosion other than the theory put forward by Mr Dan Morgan, the mine manager, that the tapping of the straw to get the powder down had resulted in a small amount being spilt and when the deceased had snuffed out his candle, a spark had somehow fallen into the spilt powder which in turn had ignited the powder in the box

Regarding the question of an open powder box being taken into the mine, the coroner was informed that the Secretary of State responsible for mines had permitted an exemption to the regulations.

Mr Dan Morgan advised the inquest that Edward Emery was an experienced miner who had worked at the mine for some ten years and 'was one of the most trustworthy men in the mine'.

Reporting on the inquest the *Shepton Mallet Journal* of 24 February 1893 wrote that the jury returned the unanimous verdict that 'The deceased died from the effects of an accidental explosion of gunpowder' and gave their fees to Edward Emery's widow, left with a family of seven children.

THE YEOVIL CHEESE ROBBERY AND OTHER CASES

Two cheeses valued at five shillings were stolen from Jane Corry at the Yeovil Market under the Town Hall on High Street during the evening of 13 January 1854, and three teenagers went to gaol.

The three, sixteen-years-old John Collins, George Vincent, fifteen, and William Sylvester, aged sixteen, appeared at the Somerset Quarter Sessions during the following March charged with stealing two cheeses the property of Jane Corry.

The said Jane told the court that she had purchased 68 cheeses at the market, but not being able to remove them all at once, she had found two missing on her return to collect those which remained.

Police Constable Trimby testified that he had been on duty at the market and observed the three youths acting in a suspicious manner. Suspecting 'something was wrong', he watched them and saw Collins and another boy, whom he could not identify in the low light, go into the market and carry away the cheeses. Vincent and Sylvester were 'hanging around' near the entrance. The constable stated that he had apprehended Collins with the cheese in his possession, and a second was found near the entrance. Collins, Vincent and Sylvester were arrested and charged with stealing the two cheeses.

All three pleaded guilty, Vincent, described as 'an old offender' was sentenced to four years penal servitude, Sylvester who had previous 'form', to two years, and Collins to two months in gaol.

Market day in Yeovil in the early 1900s, a scene probably little changed since the three teenagers were charged with stealing two cheeses in 1854.

When he saw Joseph Mitchell, junior, jumping his horse over a wall and into a field of mowing grass at Long Load, owned by his employer Mr Benjafield, Joseph Tucker scrambled up onto the wall and shouted to the young man to stop. Joseph Mitchell, however, jumped his horse over the wall again but fell off in the process. Remounting, he rode across the field but then turned and riding up to Joseph Tucker, knocked him off the wall, encouraged by his father, also Joseph by name, who had been watching the proceedings, and who shouted out 'Put it into him, put it into him! Pay him, pay him!'

The events of that afternoon were described by Joseph Tucker at the County Petty Sessions in Yeovil on 4 July 1860, when the two Mitchells appeared charged with assault and found guilty, each being fined £1 plus costs.

At the same July sitting, Ann Denty was summoned on a complaint by Sarah Higgins, following a dispute over a swarm of bees of which Sarah had 'taken possession', but which Ann claimed to be hers. Sarah Higgins alleged that Ann had hit her with a stick, but in return, Ann stated that the complainant had thrown the contents of a bucket of water in her face. The magistrates, however, took the view that this was a private row, and at their suggestion, the case was settled between the two ladies.

Likewise, at the suggestion of the magistrates, a case of assault at Chiselborough involving Jonathan Higgins and Noah Langdon was settled between the two 'disputants'.

Some thirty-one years later, on 17 January 1891, William Short, appeared at the County Petty Sessions in Yeovil, charged with stealing two fowls valued at five shillings, the property of George Cole, farmer of Yeovil Marsh.

Farmer Cole told the court that he had discovered two of his fowls were missing on the morning of 10 January, and suspicion had fallen on his former employee, William Short. Two police constables had gone to William Short's house on Coppice Hill, where they found a partly cooked fowl in a boiler over the fire, and in the back-kitchen, a second was found already plucked, together with a basket of feathers. Farmer Cole had identified the feathers as being similar to those of the stolen fowls. The court was told that the prisoner had said 'You won't be hard with me, it's my first time.'

William Short pleaded guilty stating that he had stolen the fowls because he had been out of work and his wife and family had nothing to eat. Farmer Cole told the court that William had been a good workman, and gave him an excellent character asking the magistrates to 'deal with him leniently, this being his first offence'.

The magistrates, taking in consideration that he had been in custody for nearly a week and leniency had been asked, discharged William Short hoping that 'it would be a caution to him for the future'.

AND FINALLY, THE LAST SURPRISE

And finally, it may come as something of a surprise to many people and especially the dwellers in the Emerald Isle, that the gentle haunting lyrics of the well-loved ballad 'Danny Boy', set to the old Irish tune 'A Londonderry Air', were written in 1910 by a son of Somerset, Mr Frederick Edward Weatherly. Born in Portishead, in 1848, Frederick Weatherly, was a lawyer and a King's Counsel and wrote over 3000 songs, including the popular song of the First World War – 'Roses of Picardy'.

Frederick Weatherley KC, a son of Somerset who wrote the haunting lyrics of 'Danny Boy'.

SOURCES

The following sources have been consulted in the research and preparation of this publication:

Jack W. Sweet – *Shocking Somerset Murders of the Nineteenth Century,* Somerset Books (1997 and reprint 2002), *Shocking and Surprising Somerset Stories,* Somerset Books (1999), *More Shocking and Surprising Somerset Stories,* Somerset Books (2002).

The newspapers quoted in the text and the *Western Gazette.*

Jack W Sweet's private papers.

ACKNOWLEDGEMENTS

My great appreciation and thanks to the editor of the *Western Gazette* for permission to use the articles from The *Western Gazette* in this book. And a very special thanks to my great friend Allan Collier for his help in research for *Lawrence of the RAF.*

All the images used in this publication are from the author's private collection.

Every effort has been made to contact the copyright holders but please contact the publisher if you are aware of any omissions, which will be rectified in any future editions.